How to
AVOID
ALIMONY

by
Maurice R. Franks

A SIGNET BOOK
NEW AMERICAN LIBRARY
TIMES MIRROR

Library of Congress Catalog Card Number: 75-14231

This is an authorized reprint of a hardcover edition published
by Saturday Review Press. The hardcover edition was published
simultaneously in Canada by Clarke, Irwin & Company Limited,
Toronto and Vancouver.

SIGNET TRADEMARK REG. U.S. PAT. OFF. AND FOREIGN COUNTRIES
REGISTERED TRADEMARK—MARCA REGISTRADA
HECHO EN CHICAGO, U.S.A.

SIGNET, SIGNET CLASSICS, MENTOR, PLUME AND MERIDIAN BOOKS
are published by The New American Library, Inc.,
1301 Avenue of the Americas, New York, New York 10019

FIRST SIGNET PRINTING, NOVEMBER, 1976

1 2 3 4 5 6 7 8 9

PRINTED IN THE UNITED STATES OF AMERICA

It is with deepest gratitude that I pay respects to the force that was of immeasurable assistance to me in the making of this book:

To the steady incentive provided me by

MY WIFE,

who shall remain nameless, and her attorney, who likewise shall remain nameless, for their repeated unsuccessful attempts to force me to pay alimony.

Without their help, the idea of this book never would have been conceived.

Acknowledgment

With more sincere gratitude, I acknowledge the assistance given me by D. Donald Donato, a friend and a journalist, for his editorial help in the translation of "legalese" into the reality and readable English of *How to Avoid Alimony*.

Contents

PREFACE

You are probably holding this book fearing you have just been cheated out of some money your wife is trying to take away from you.

Well, relax. I've been down the same road. The only difference between us is that I'm a lawyer—and my wife did not get all of my money.

She didn't get my house, either. She didn't get the two motor vehicles or my three cabins in the mountains. She did get a refrigerator.

Right about now, you're probably muttering something like, "But *you* are an attorney, and I'm not."

Consider the situation: Would I waste my time writing a book about how to avoid paying alimony if it weren't going to help the non-attorney?

If the plans had no chance of working, then word would get around pretty fast. And, when the word got around, just how many books would I sell?

I might be able to give away a few copies to my true friends, but nobody else would want one of the damn things around catching dust!

The system worked for me, and it might work for you.

The reason it worked is quite simple. It's based on the laws of the United States.

Contrary to what you might be thinking with a divorce suit staring you in the face, the laws of this country were not designed to punish you for being alive. Quite the opposite. The laws were meant to protect your rights to life, liberty and the pursuit of happiness.

Actually, men owe a great deal to the women's liberation movement. After all, the women's movement pointed out that men and women are equal under the law.

Historically, in divorce cases the man is always wrong and should be punished severely unless his wife is an active prostitute (and he is not a pimp).

That's exactly the indication according to the majority of the rulings. The man has to support the woman, because she is a helpless creature—and besides, that's the way it's always been done.

That's what one finds reading old divorce cases. However, women's liberation has proven that females are not helpless or witless or even in some cases poor.

In 1868, the Fourteenth Amendment was ratified, proclaiming ". . . nor shall any State . . . deny to any person within its jurisdiction the equal protection of the laws."

In 1972, the U.S. Supreme Court suggested that the equal-protection clause of the Fourteenth Amendment requires the states to treat the sexes equally.

Women have emphasized for us the equality of the sexes.

If one digs far enough back into legal history, he finds another interesting approach that appears to make quite a bit of sense.

It seems that as of 1865, involuntary servitude—slavery—became illegal in this great land, with ratification of the Thirteenth Amendment.

Concerning involuntary servitude—peonage in legal terms, and plain old working to support a woman after you aren't married to her anymore, in English—a civil rights law passed in 1867 (42 U.S. Code § 1994) in part provides:

> The holding of any person to service or labor under the system known as peonage is abolished and forever prohibited in any Territory or State of the United States. . . .

Now, you probably see the direction we have been

going. I sort of led you around the garden for two reasons:

The first reason was, hopefully, to get your interest and to let you know I'm on your side.

The second reason was to let you in on a very well-kept secret. That is: Simply because your wife wants a divorce *does not* mean you must work like a Siberian slave until the time she might or might not graciously decide to remarry and let you off the hook.

Contrary to what some judges seem to think, you have rights, too. In fact, you have the same rights your wife has.

And that is the whole point of this book. I took my own case all the way to the United States Supreme Court. You can too, if necessary.

When I say "you," actually, I mean your attorney can. Oh, sure, 28 U.S. Code § 1654 says you have an absolute right to represent yourself in federal court.

In most states, you also legally could represent yourself in the divorce court. Using the methods in this book, you probably could commence your own suit in federal court.

It would be doomed to fail.

Although you might have the right to represent yourself, the existence of that right does not automatically clothe you in the armor of experience and courtroom savvy your wife's attorney will have gained by hours of study and years of actually appearing before the bench.

I realize I'm bursting one of your bubbles.

Just so there will be no misunderstanding, I'll say it plainer—get yourself a lawyer. You'll need his expertise. But, don't get stung. Get one who will really work for you.

Hiring a good attorney is so important that it is covered in the second chapter. Read that chapter carefully, and with what it says firmly in mind, read the rest of the book.

Then, go out and find an attorney like the one described in Chapter II. Then have him read this book. If he's really the man (or for that matter, woman) you want, he might already have read this book.

This book is intended to inform and not give advice or general solutions applicable to all apparently similar problems. Laws vary widely from state to state. No person ever should attempt to apply or interpret any law without the aid of a trained expert who knows the facts, because slight differences in the facts may require a material variance in the applicable advice.

That and the simple fact that you can't cram law school and courtroom experience into any book is the reason a truly smart man will hire an attorney.

"Women's liberation
is truly the liberation
of all people."
    —Gerald R. Ford

Chapter VII

How to
AVOID
ALIMONY

Chapter I

HOW I GOT INVOLVED

It all came together one lonely night in Westcliffe—eight thousand feet up in the Colorado Rocky Mountains—as I sat in the local honky-tonk pizza house, brushing the flies away, eating a pizza and not hearing the jukebox.

Like a forgotten record on the turntable, the recent, painful journey to aloneness replayed and replayed . . .

Like something from an Italian movie, it had begun with a lavish birthday party prepared for me by my wife. A very nice party it was, with cake and candles and friends.

Floating, filled with goodwill for my fellow man, enjoying the budding high-country spring, the next day I headed for business appointments in Denver. I was still full of goodwill when I returned home and found that my wife had moved out.

It was, to say the least, a shock. I'd had no idea she was unhappy.

Suddenly, she was living in a motel room in town . . . and when I found her, she wanted a divorce. Just like that.

At the time my wife was teaching in the local school. Because only a few months remained until classes would be over for the summer, I suggested a cooling-off period.

I wanted her to think about this seemingly sudden

1

decision. I said, "If you'll wait until the end of the school year, and if you still want a divorce, I'll give you one without a contest."

She said she would wait . . . and the next day she hired a lawyer and got the first divorce papers filed.

I flew to New Jersey and brought her parents back with me to Colorado—at my expense—so they could take her out of the environment and away from some of the influences I thought might be affecting her.

Her parents took her and nothing was accomplished there. She filed a motion for temporary maintenance and for attorney fees, and she asked for a division of property. Her motion for temporary alimony was all she and her lawyer could ask for in the way of support because permanent alimony was ruled out by a premarital agreement.

Sitting in the little café, I was pondering my future, and remembered arriving at the judge's chambers to set a date for hearing of her motion for temporary maintenance. The judge turned to me and asked, "Mr. Franks, how come you aren't supporting your wife? Is it your position you are under no obligation to support your wife?"

I saw the probable direction the case was headed. It didn't take me long to resolve that her motion would never be heard in that court.

My thoughts turned even farther back, to when I was law clerk for the Louisiana Supreme Court; to my work as an assistant district attorney for "Big Jim" Garrison in New Orleans. After about four months of trial work for him, he put me in charge of a stack of federal cases. They included not only habeas corpus cases, but also civil rights suits for money damages which had been brought against the district attorney's office and other officials in New Orleans.

Perhaps fleeing the problem of the hour, my brain calmly noted that some of those New Orleans suits raised interesting and novel questions—New Orleans is a hotbed for some of the best civil rights lawyers in the country.

One of the suits was from a murder case that was removed from state court to federal court on the ground that the defendant was "racially prejudiced against" because he was something like one-thirty-second part American Indian.

Which was totally frivolous—would be even in Colorado.

And in Louisiana, nobody discriminates against American Indians: that's just not the group discriminated against in Louisiana. Of course there are groups that are, but that's not one of them. Many Louisianians, you see, are part American Indian. "Big-Toe Indians," they call them in Oklahoma. That is to say, they have enough American Indian blood in them to fill their big toe.

Scientists tell us the unconscious never rests. In its ramblings that mountain summer night, my unconscious mind showed me that because of my work with cases of the New Orleans type, I was somewhat familiar with federal civil procedure and its possibilities. Having defended some far-out federal suits, I understood civil rights theories.

Also, going back to law school, I recalled work as law clerk for a professor with two Ph.D.s (one of them from Cambridge) who wrote the briefs for most of the Southern states in the voting rights cases back in the 1960s—defending what I since have come to regard as pure bigotry.

My background, I found that night, has always included an intense interest in the U.S. Constitution and in peoples' rights under the Constitution.

The pizza wasn't going very fast, but my thoughts were like a child hopping from rock to rock, crossing and recrossing a quick-flowing stream.

Back I went to the judge's chambers and the first hearing to pick a date. I suggested (most naïvely, I since have learned) something along the line that men who are able to get a job but refuse to do so get jailed, whereas women who are able to get a job but refuse to do so get alimony.

The judge said, "I've heard that one before."

And that brought to mind concepts of right and wrong, fair and unfair—and an article I'd read on women's rights in *Case & Comment,* a legal magazine. In connection with that, I thought and thought about my own case again—and came up with the obvious facts of sexual discrimination and slavery as objections to the typical manner in which divorce courts handle divorce cases.

Another motivating factor was that after my wife had filed her suit—which she had agreed not to file under our informal cooling-off period—she offered a list of items that she wanted. A lot of these were her personal items, her undisputed personal items; but *some* of the things on that list, I felt, were not proper.

She wanted the records, and to the best of my knowledge she owned only a small number of LPs and I had a fairly substantial (not gigantic) record collection acquired prior to the marriage.

Anyway, I had hired a lawyer—oh, yes, I hired a lawyer in Canon City, where the case then was pending, on the premise that a lawyer, like anybody else, should be represented by counsel. I drew up a new property list and struck off very few items from my wife's list.

Back came a letter to my lawyer from my wife's attorney. It read:

   I have received a reply from Mrs. Franks and she absolutely refuses to change the list of items regarding personal property. My instructions are to insist upon the original list remaining unchanged. She is without work and has further instructed me to seek additional support for her along with a share of other real and personal property if Mr. Franks doesn't agree to the implementation of our original offer.

At which point I figured, "Come ahead, baby, just try."

Addressing a pizza-loving fly, I asked why, if I had to go through this again, couldn't it at least go like my first marriage's demise? At eighteen I was married the first time. It was a teenage marriage and it didn't work out, but it ended nicely. Now, this one . . .

This marriage ended in circumstances under which I felt fully justified in taking a hard-nosed attitude. I will not go into all the details. The question in my mind as I fought the flies for my pizza was whether to go to Puerto Rico, where my wife's parents had taken her, and file an action against her in the courts there?

Among the choices racing through my mind, I was weighing what amounted to probably eighty dollars a month for alimony for three months—total, two hundred and forty—and the opposite course, in this case the much larger expense of handling the litigation of opposing any alimony.

A toast given in 1798 at a banquet for Chief Justice John Marshall came to me: "Millions for defense, but not one cent for tribute!" Suddenly my thoughts crystallized—under the particular circumstances of this case, I'd had all I could take without fighting back.

One cent of alimony was one cent too much!

Slamming my can of Coors on the table, startling the hell out of several cowmen, my decision was made—"Damn it, no, I am not going to yield!"

How to carry the battle to my wife—now my opponent?

I am an attorney. I chose legal weapons. I went back home, packed the bag, typed up some pleadings very quickly, took the next plane to San Juan, and filed in the United States District Court for Puerto Rico.

I got excellent reception from the officials there in

terms of courtesy and cordiality, in finding a local lawyer to help with the filings, and in getting a local U.S. marshal to head out into the night across the mountains of Puerto Rico through a storm to serve the papers because my wife was probably going to return to Colorado at any moment, since the alimony hearing was only a few days off.

That deputy marshal deserves some credit. The mountains of Puerto Rico are more difficult to cross on the fifty miles from San Juan to the other side of the island than any mountain pass I know of in Colorado.

The marshal served the papers on my wife just before she left Puerto Rico. She was not happy about it, the man said.

Later, back in Colorado, it became apparent the suit in Puerto Rico was not moving. So I filed a writ in the Colorado Supreme Court to enjoin the local court from proceeding, on the ground that the Puerto Rico federal suit automatically divested the state courts of jurisdiction.

My thinking was based on the case of *United Services Life Insurance Co.* v. *Delaney,* which is a Texas case holding that when a federal court has a case pending between the same parties involving the same questions, the state courts may not proceed.

In *Delaney,* the federal court said: We will stay proceedings because we want to hear what the Texas state courts have to say on this. The Supreme Court of Texas, however, said: No, we cannot tell you what we have to say on this because once the same questions have been presented to a federal court, the federal court has the case. We cannot move until the federal case is adjudicated to final disposition.

The Texas Supreme Court, not because of any injunction from a federal court, but rather by a doctrine of commendable self-restraint, admitted that it didn't have jurisdiction. Which means that in Texas, a federal three-judge-panel suit (more about that later) should operate to jam the state-court proceedings, as it does not automatically do in Colorado.

The Colorado Supreme Court denied the writ.

I filed suit in the United States District Court for the District of Colorado against the state divorce judge. I also named as defendants my wife, and Colorado's at-that-time-Governor John Vanderhoof, and the then-Attorney-General John P. Moore. I asked the federal court to restrain them and the trial court from violating my rights in any way.

The trial judge reacted by withdrawing himself from the case, thus making it necessary for the Colorado Supreme Court to appoint a new judge to hear the divorce. The Chief Justice of the state high court eventually appointed a judge from Salida to try the case.

I was prepared: I asked the United States District Court to enjoin the state district court from proceeding to trial. I also asked that the case be certified for hearing by a panel of three judges and for prompt treatment as a constitutional case. The case was so certified.

When the Chief Judge of the United States Court of Appeals appointed a distinguished three-judge panel to hear the case, the state judge at Salida seemed to lose interest in hearing the divorce before the federal court could rule on the matter.

My wife's attorney wrote me a letter indicating that he would be willing to negotiate. I had the satisfaction of sending him a photocopy of his own letter—the one indicating that there would be no negotiation.

In December 1973, the three-judge panel heard arguments on whether to enjoin the state court. They handed down an interesting decision in which they declined to enjoin the state proceedings—but made it explicit that the federal door remained open for later on in my case. They stayed the federal suit.

The federal court said that since the courts of Colorado had never in the past ruled on these particular questions, they should be given a first opportunity to rule. The federal court explicitly stated that a ruling by the state courts upholding my position would make federal intervention unnecessary.

Still, I didn't want the case tried in state court—I didn't have as much faith as did the federal court—so I took an appeal to the Supreme Court of the United States. The only issue on appeal was the correctness of the decision of the federal court declining to proceed further until the state courts had an opportunity to rule.

Standing in the U.S. Supreme Court building, one gets an exhilarating sensation of justice, a feeling of confidence in the judicial system—a sensation singularly absent in the lackluster atmosphere of many county courthouses across the nation.

It is an awe-inspiring court.

I'd been to the U.S. Supreme Court before, but not in person—only by mail for the New Orleans district attorney's office, which is not at all the same.

The U.S. Supreme Court upheld the action of the federal court in staying federal proceedings pending state court determination. My appeal was dismissed for lack of jurisdiction, with Mr. Justice Douglas dissenting from the dismissal of the appeal.

I don't know how many of the other justices voted in my favor. The practice is not to note dissents on memorandum decisions of the Supreme Court. Only on full decisions do they normally note dissents. It is unusual for a justice to note his dissent to a memorandum decision such as mine. Mr. Justice Douglas evidently felt strongly enough, though, to do so.

The state divorce court now apparently was ready to proceed. I argued some motions at Salida. That was when my wife's attorney apparently got the idea that it would be wise to abandon any attempts at alimony. They formally dropped their demands for alimony. The plan had worked.

The court then set the case for trial. At trial, the

court proceeded to divide the marital property, giving my wife her clothing, her undisputed personal belongings, and—the refrigerator. And some other stuff too inconsequential to mention. I even kept the pots and dishes.

I'm just getting to the point that I can appreciate the victory instead of pondering imponderables. The case has had its benefits. I've kept my property, and have developed what I call the "federal approach" for fighting a divorce suit. One option to the approach absolutely will jam the state-court divorce suit.

How about that? Because my wife left me, I have discovered, and since refined, methods of using the federal approach to bring a divorce suit to a screeching halt. And the methods should continue to work for so long as state divorce courts treat men differently because of their sex.

The simple, very, very legal approach points out that neither the federal court in which the action is filed nor the state court from which the divorce is being removed has jurisdiction!

Chapter II

GET A LAWYER!

This book is designed to help the man who is faced with divorce, but who thinks his wife shouldn't be able just to walk into an attorney's office and take away everything.

In some divorce cases, "everything" turns out to mean *everything* the couple owned jointly. About all the man gets out of the proceeding is his clothing. Oh, yes, and he gets all the bills and a warning from the court that if he doesn't maintain the woman in a style to which she would like to become accustomed, he will go to jail.

The steel shackles and iron bars of bondage are every bit as real to the male slaves of the twentieth century as they were to their black counterparts of the nineteenth.

This entire book was written with a goal in mind. That goal is to help men get a fair shake in their divorce cases—to make men aware that under the laws of the United States, men have the right not to pay alimony or outrageous child support.

To repeat, get a lawyer.

There are monetary dangers in representing yourself in court. It's sort of like walking blindfolded through a minefield in which every mine has a big, bright, red spot on its top. If you weren't wearing the blindfold, you could see the red dots and you easily could avoid the mines.

In the courtroom, an attorney has the advantage. He isn't wearing a blindfold and can see the red dots, but you, without law training and experience, are blindfolded. As you blunder around the legal minefield, your wife's attorney can beat you out of the field, while you may lose everything you've worked for in your entire life.

Even though you might understand the constitutional issues involved, the lawyer on the other side will be able to take technical advantage of you by using court procedural rules you don't know exist.

Because you probably don't know how to use a law library and its complicated system of indexing, you will be unable to do the research needed to fight objections by your wife's attorney and by the attorney general of your state.

The odds are high (damn high) that you will inadvertently step over the thin line that divides effective representation from contempt of court.

You see, part of the method outlined in this book involves suing your local judge in federal court.

After you've done that, the average man in the black robes will be none too tolerant of any mistakes you might make. And, under those circumstances, any mistake you make will be noticed and brought painfully to your attention—even if the judge might let your wife's lawyer get away with it.

If you're too poor to afford a lawyer, you might try filing your own suit in federal court, along with a motion (request) for leave to proceed as a pauper (that is, as a poor person—which is how many women file for divorce).

If you do this, you will need to file an affidavit, a sworn statement, that you are unable to pay court costs or to afford an attorney, and ask the court to relieve you from having to pay court costs and to appoint a lawyer for you. While the right to proceed as a pauper without paying court costs is firmly established, there is not yet any right to a court-appointed lawyer in a civil case. Some courts will appoint counsel for indigents in civil suits, and some will not.

If your local court has a rule permitting poor female defendants in divorce cases to get court-appointed counsel, then sexual equality as guaranteed under the equal protection clause of the Fourteenth Amendment would seem to dictate that male defendants should get the same break. If you can't afford a good attorney, then a motion to the state court to appoint counsel for you would seem appropriate.

But, if you are out to win—that is, to save some of that property you worked for and will work for in the future—it might be best to avoid court-appointed lawyers.

Competent private representation is infinitely superior to representation by a court-appointed lawyer. In many cases the court may appoint someone who is not at all familiar with constitutional law or with civil rights law. And that is what your case is all about— the U.S. Constitution and civil rights!

With respect to your divorce suit in state court, you won't even get to first base trying to use the methods in this book, simply because procedures vary so widely from one state to another. Of course, the lawyer you hire probably won't get to first base in state court, either, but at least he should be able to protect and preserve your rights for assertion in (that is, to go on to) federal court.

Even if you cannot afford a lawyer, you still may be able to find some eager civil rights lawyer who will represent you without charge.

The attorney you're looking for is young, brilliant, and aggressive. He probably graduated in the top 20 percent of his class.

The lawyer you want has guts. He won't be on the payroll of any of the bigger law firms. Rarely will the underlings, or anyone else in a giant law firm, touch anything controversial.

The lawyer you're looking for has been out of law school about two years. In those two years he's been smart enough to gain all the experience you'll need him to have. And he hasn't yet lost his youthful enthusiasm and willingness to tackle the unusual.

He may be the only lawyer in town with enough nerve to handle a suit against the local police department. And the policemen may hate him. But, they'll respect him. And—most likely—he's the lawyer the cops would use if they needed a lawyer and were free to choose their own without having to go through city hall.

The lawyer you want appears regularly and often on behalf of people injured in automobile accidents.

He or she is not afraid to go to trial.

The one you want is in private practice, and enjoys handling civil rights cases.

Find out, by reputation, who this lawyer is, and you've found the one you want. Ask around. Ask other lawyers.

Why the big deal about picking a lawyer?

Bar associations uniformly maintain the fiction that all lawyers are equally competent in all areas of the law, with the minor exceptions of patent law and maritime law. The associations claim bar examinations keep incompetents from entering the profession in the first place, and that those few who do slip through are quickly weeded out by disbarment proceedings.

False!

Not too many years ago, in many states, it was possible to be admitted to practice without ever having to take a bar exam. The law-school diploma was all the proof the bar examiners wanted. Many older lawyers were admitted on this basis. They never have taken a bar exam.

Indeed, the "diploma privilege" still hangs on. It's

still possible to get a law license without having to take even a token bar examination in Wisconsin, West Virginia, Mississippi, and Montana.

Some states have always admitted only by bar examination. However, until recent years, in many places the bar examination was a mere formality. Nearly everyone passed. Even today, bar examinations are still comparatively easy in states such as Idaho, Nebraska, North Dakota, South Dakota, and South Carolina. A favorite trick a few years ago was to take the bar exam in an "easy" state and then apply for admission in the desired state on reciprocity (that is, you're licensed in one state, so why not the other), thereby avoiding having to take the tougher test in the state in which you really want to practice.

Generally, requirements for a law license are being stiffened all the time. Most of the younger lawyers have had to meet these somewhat tougher requirements. But, over the years, many a dolt has been given a law license. Each year, more than a few still slip through.

On the other hand, only a handful of lawyers are disbarred for incompetence each year. The incompetence generally must be *gross,* and it must be proven to the satisfaction of the bar association's ethics-and-grievance committee. Of those few who are caught, many are merely reprimanded for their stupidity; few ever lose their license for anything less than blatant dishonesty.

Also, just because an attorney is competent does not mean that he is a hard worker. It doesn't mean he is willing to exert that extra effort needed to win a client's case.

To be perfectly honest, most lawyers are frightened at the thought of having to face a federal court. And they would almost rather sell pencils on a street corner than do the library research necessary to write an appellate brief. The problem is that they may know the law, but their familiarity with the mechanics and procedure of convening a three-judge federal panel are about as great as your own. Most lawyers won't admit this, but it's true.

Then, the thought of striking down your state's divorce law as unconstitutional is less than attractive to most attorneys, who are making plenty of money under the current setup.

Now, just for spice (and because it will be necessary in the federal-action part of your suit if you opt in favor of going for a three-judge court) we'll mention the prospect of suing the governor and attorney general of your state.

The very idea will scare away the lightweights.

And then the thought of suing your local trial judge in federal court will surely scare off all but the toughest, most competent lawyers.

When the attorney you propose to hire labels the suggestions in this book "impractical," he really may be thinking to himself, "What will Judge Green think? Will this alienate him? Will he like me anymore?"

The answers are, of course, pretty obvious. Judges are human—don't look so surprised; it's true! You bet it will alienate the judge! But then, Judge Green probably doesn't like you or your lawyer, anyhow. So why not go ahead?

Who's going to pay the alimony if you don't win your case? Judge Green?

When the federal suit is all over, Judge Green probably still won't like you. But he will have acquired a new respect for you and for your lawyer. You and your lawyer both win twice. You might keep your house, and when your lawyer appears before Judge Green again, the good judge will handle *that* attorney with respect and kid gloves!

No extensive research is necessary, because it's all been done in advance for your lawyer. All your attorney need do is modify the methods outlined in this book to fit his analysis of the particular facts of your case and to fit the differences in local law peculiar to your state.

His secretary then will type up the papers for filing with the court.

The filing fee in federal court is fifteen dollars. But unless you are represented by the legal-aid office, it may cost you one or two thousand dollars to hire a good lawyer. This is cheap compared to a lifetime of outrageous alimony.

You can hire a lawyer on an hourly basis for an amount ranging anywhere from twenty to about one hundred and fifty dollars an hour. Or you and he can agree in advance on a flat fee for handling your case. Since you'll be asking your lawyer to file a large number of motions, the flat fee might be your best bet in the long run. If the case bogs down, the hourly rate will run up and up. But the flat rate, though possibly larger-sounding on the front end, will take care of the entire case for one lump sum. Make sure you get a clear understanding of what the flat fee will include.

After you've gotten the lawyer to agree to take a "fee certain," get him to agree to take it in installments. Lawyers usually will go along with this. Say the attorney agrees to handle your case for $1000. Give him a retainer of $250 this month and pay him $250 each month for the next three months, or some similar arrangement that will fit your budget.

Most lawyers will not charge interest, although a recent opinion of the American Bar Association's Standing Committee on Ethics and Professional Responsibility now allows attorneys to charge interest on delinquent accounts if the client agrees.

It really is no more difficult for your lawyer to type and file motions in federal court than in state court. Unless you live outside a metropolitan area, it is no further to the federal courthouse than to your county courthouse. Yet lawyers customarily charge higher fees for filing in federal court than they do for filing in state court. There really isn't any legitimate reason for this, except that federal judges tend to be less tolerant of sloppy workmanship than most state judges.

In federal court, your lawyer had better be prepared. While many state judges are reluctant to dress down attorneys in the presence of their clients, most federal judges have no similar inhibitions.

So, get a lawyer. Be picky. Remember how your mother used to choose vegetables at the market? Be that picky! Your choice (just like Mom's efforts) may determine just how well you eat in the future.

Remember—50 percent of the lawyers in this country graduated in the bottom half of their class.

Chapter III

FICTION—AND WHY

The three chapters following this one are fiction. That is to say, all the people in the chapters are imaginary. Any resemblance to any real person, living or dead, or to any real person's name, is purely coincidental.

The people in the three chapters are stereotypical of persons who appear regularly in divorce actions all over the country. Just as policemen use composite drawings of suspects (and I cast no aspersions on anyone), I have used composites of some of the extremes found where divorces are taking place. Everywhere.

For men facing divorce, or who fear they soon might be, the chapters offer three radically different profiles with which to compare themselves. Few persons will fit firmly into the mold of any of these three, but each of us may find a place somewhere in between.

The fact that a man can fit his own case into the framework of the three fictitious families should be reassuring to a degree. Often men facing or involved in divorces feel they are alone, the only ones ever to have experienced their divorce-inciting circumstances.

Actually, of the three fiction chapters, the first (Mr. and Mrs. Smith) is by far the least likely to be found in real life. Even the wealthy manage to have squalid divorces. They usually, however, manage to hide the dirty linen in the closets of huge law firms. But we can't overlook the fact that there truly are persons so civilized that they can calmly, dispassionately, and totally without rancor discuss and consummate their divorces.

However, there are more of the other two kinds of divorces—the Browns' and Joneses'—when we speak in very general terms, of course.

Divorce is one of those areas overabundantly supplied with misinformation, reinforced by stereotypes. To stress this, I have used stereotyped characters, doing the stereotyped-divorce things.

One of the interesting things about divorce is that it is an area in which the wildest stereotyping goes unnoticed from day to day in attorneys' offices and in judges' chambers and courtrooms. Perhaps the cruelest aspect from the male point of view is that the stereotyping in divorce cases has fostered a mistaken belief (among the men and women in the street, among attorneys, and even among those who should know better—judges) that divorce cases are being handled fairly and according to the law.

As you read the fiction chapters, you may not appreciate which portions are indicative of the stereotyping that does in fact occur—but which also is illegal. Those stereotypes have been included. By the time you finish reading this book, you should be able to recognize those and other unconstitutional but traditional approaches to handling divorce.

In summation, the fiction chapters were written to be illustrative. They also were written to be informative—directly, and indirectly, since they will be referred to in later chapters. The reader will be able to refer back to them at book's end and apply the theories he has learned to each of the fictional cases.

As you read the three chapters that follow, remember: The Smiths have made it; the Browns and Joneses, however, are headed for typical divorces in which the man gets shafted—a grievous injustice that might be avoided.

Chapter IV

THE SMITHS

They're sitting in the living room, cups of coffee balanced on their knees; a tremendous view of the city is seen through the spotless picture window. John and Beatrice Smith are discussing their own divorce.

No passion creeps into their voices. Of course, that's one of the problems in their marriage. "Yes, John, I think that has to be one of the major difficulties. We are simply not passionate any longer," Bea comments thoughtfully.

John and Bea are nearing middle age. They have been married for fourteen years. John is well educated and is well-to-do because he is an excellent architect. Bea is well educated and well-to-do because her father was kind enough to leave her a bundle when he passed on.

The children are bright, used to good living, not used to household chores, and have had their teeth straightened. John Jr. is thirteen, and Gertrude is eleven. They already have been told of the impending divorce. Naturally, they are taking it quite well.

After all, it's not as if crockery had been dashed against the elegant wallpaper. Everything has been arranged so intelligently and calmly, what is there not to take well?

Last week—Tuesday, it was—they went to the family attorney. Old Smedley was rather taken aback.

Not so much by the divorce idea itself, but by the more outrageous proposal that he represent both husband and wife.

"Unheard of!" he roared in his best trial voice. "Just isn't done! I mean to say, who's going to look after the best interests of whichever of you I don't represent while I'm representing both of you? Eh? Puzzle me that, if you can!"

Finally, they calmed him. Of course he again was decidedly uncalm when they explained that the divorce was all planned—Bea would get the house in town and the station wagon and would live off the interest from her inherited stocks and bonds, and John would get the fishing lodge and the Mercedes and would pay for the tuition and so forth for the children.

"But, that," Smedley thundered once more, "is what you hire an attorney for! I'm supposed to see that whomever of you I represent doesn't get fleeced!"

John gently lowered Smedley's outstretched-arm-with-finger-pointing, and lowered the old gentleman firmly into his swivel chair.

"See here, Smedley," John said, reasonable as ever, "we've thought of all that. Actually, we need you for what you are good at—drawing up those endless legal papers."

"Pleadings!" snorted Smedley, momentarily forgetting the initial assault upon the bastions of attorneyism.

"Yes, well, pleadings, then. At any rate, we need you to oversee the paperwork. We've got the details all written out here. I had my secretary type them up so they'd be legible. We need you, Smedley, as our counselor and family friend, to put them into acceptable form."

Smedley still didn't look too thrilled by the whole idea.

"And, of course," John continued, "we have considered the problem of a fee in this type of thing. With no real court battle and all, it might be hard to decide what to charge us. So, we checked into the matter and found that often the fees are based upon a percentage of the property division or some such. Would ten thousand be fair, do you think?"

"Oh, much more than fair," Smedley agreed.

"Good," Bea said with obvious relief. "How soon can we get on with it then, do you think?"

Well, with those months of planning, Beatrice and John had pretty well covered the entire field. The ten-thousand fee in advance hadn't slowed the process, either.

John's belongings were moved to his rented house two blocks down and one to the south yesterday. The trial-but-final separation begins today.

"John?"

"Um, yes, Bea?"

"You won't forget to call if you're going to be late for dinner, will you?"

"You know I always call if I'll be late," he smiled.

"Yes, I guess I do . . ." He'd gotten her on that one, and she too smiled. "Well, then we'll expect you about seven, and I do hope the bakery sends a nice cake for John Jr.'s birthday party."

John stands up, pats her affectionately on the shoulder, clears the bowl of his pipe, and stuffs the hand-worn briar into his suitcoat pocket. "Well, best be off. You know how Simpson is if I'm not there to approve his latest plans by eleven."

"Yes, I know. Drive carefully."

With a cheery wave to the picture window, he climbs into his Mercedes and guides it down the winding street just as he's guided the divorce proceedings. Carefully, and with an even temper.

Chapter V

BOB AND FLO

The man behind the desk is short, bald under the stepped-on-looking hat he wears to try and hide the fact; he is greasy-pudgy fat, and smells of stale sweat, not honest-work oniony.

Arny Gurns looks like a two-bit bookie, or like what he really is—an average, pretty-good, quasi-legal private detective.

Drawing on his cheap cigar in apparent delight, Gurns studies his client.

The information is delivered in a flat voice, indicating that he is not taking sides in what he is reporting—only reporting.

"Your wife, Mrs. Florence Brown—dark-brown, short hair; five feet, eight inches tall; weight about one-thirty-five; green eyes; employed as a buyer for Fashion-Rights for Women—is messing around with another man.

"The subject takes long lunch hours—sometimes two or three hours—supposedly to wine and dine clients. Clients being those ones from which the subject's company buys ladies' clothes.

"However, as near as I can figure, about four months ago the subject began taking the long lunches and not seeing no clients. However, she has kept her nose clean at the office by coming to work earlier and stay-

23

ing later. As near as I can find out, her work is of the same high quality as previously.

"During these non-business long lunches, the subject in the last four months has been seeing a male party, not her husband. These meetings take place at an apartment about a two-minute fast walk from the subject's place of employment.

"This apartment is rented to a male party by the name of Joseph Jacobs. This Joseph Jacobs being the same male party who has been seeing the subject on the long non-business lunch hours.

"It has been determined without doubt that the subject and Jacobs have been having sexual relations."

"Oh, Jesus!" Bob slumps in his chair, hands over his face. Two thoughts pound on his brain at the same time. His wife has been unfaithful to him, and the greasy, smelly slob across from his has probably witnessed the very act and probably has even enjoyed the peep show.

Gurns, guessing the other's thoughts, hurriedly continues his monologue.

"Joseph Jacobs—male caucasian; thirty-one, two years older than subject; six feet tall; weight about two-fifty-five; rust-color hair; full beard; blue eyes; artist, a—whaddaya call it—sells his own stuff . . ."

"Free-lance artist?"

"Yeh. Free-lance artist, commercial artist—met subject while trying to sell her company on some of his advertising pictures; relationship was just business until about four months ago; and the relationship now is just what I said before.

"Here's a written copy of my report, with names, dates, addresses, and expenses. Oh, yeh, and color photographs with negatives. And, don't worry, I ain't got no copies to blackmail ya with. I useta be a cop.

"This here is my bill. It's all, like you accountant guys say, itemized."

Bob pays the seventy-five dollars for the three days,

the eighteen-forty-nine for renting the surveillance room, and the twelve-fourteen for meals, and stuffs the report into his inside jacket pocket before walking out without a backward glance.

Later that afternoon, after a couple of bourbons neat, Bob Brown mechanically walks across the living room of his suburban home to answer the doorbell.

It takes him several seconds after opening the door to realize he is looking at a man in a deputy-sheriff's uniform.

"Mr. Robert L. Brown?" the officer asks noncommittally.

"Uh, yes. That's me."

The deputy holds something out, and as people will do, Brown automatically reaches out and takes it.

"Sir, it is my duty to inform you that you have been duly served with a petition for divorce proceedings in circuit court. You are hereby summoned into said court at nine-thirty A.M. on Tuesday, four June, to show cause why your wife should not be granted temporary alimony and child support, temporary custody, and exclusive use of the family home pending final dissolution of your marriage in accordance with the plaintiff's wishes."

"That's my birthday."

"I beg your pardon, sir?"

"June four. It's my birthday."

"I see, sir. Please sign your legal signature here and here. This is to support my records that you have been served in accordance with state law."

Brown's signature is shaky in both places.

As the door closes behind him, the deputy walks toward the waiting cruiser, shaking his head. "Jesus. On the guy's goddamn birthday."

Chapter VI

THEY'RE BOTH ROTTEN

The living room looks like an on-tour "Broadway show" set: a hodgepodge of antique, Danish-modern, and early-average-knickknack ungraces the middle-aged home in a no-longer-fashionable section of the city.

"I've really got you this time, crumb. I've got actual photographs!" Diane Jones is so indignantly, gleefully angry that she looks forty-five instead of only thirty-five. She pats her spray-varnished hair, which looks as if even dynamite wouldn't dislodge one strand.

Talbot Jones, her paunchy husband, takes another slug of his cheap whiskey. Ignoring the big drop that splashes through one of the holes in his food-stained undershirt, Talbot nonchalantly swings his arm up over the back of the old sofa, and snarls, "Yeh, yeh, yeh. You trying to tell me you ain't ballin' old bosso? Huh?"

"Oh, yeh? And so what if I am?" Diane unconsciously pinches the creases in her expensive pants and tucks in her slighty clashing blouse, which tells of her poor childhood. "If I am, it's kept you in money enough that *you* don't have to go out and work for a living, and so you have enough left over to chase anything with skirts on!"

Talbot runs a hand over the gray-speckled stubble on his double chins. He looks younger than Diane, which actually is not the case by several years. At length, he speaks:

"We got two kids, in case you forgot. If I didn't stay home and take care of those little guys, just who in hell would? Not you. That's for damn sure. They were an accident, even if you won't admit it. I happen to love those kids. In spite of who their mother is, they're pretty goddamn good kids."

Diane, too, is yelling. "You can have 'em, if you want those brats. What I want is the house and car, and I want you to get off your lazy butt and support *me* for a change!"

Worked into a red-froth rage, Diane storms out.

Next morning she leaves to see an attorney.

Talbot gets the twins up, feeds them breakfast with a vitamin on the side as he fixes sack lunches, and sends them off to school, as usual. Then, despite his also-usual hangover, Talbot washes the dishes and begins the endless chore of housekeeping, again, as usual.

Diane tells her story and the lawyer nods judiciously (practicing, always, for the bench someday).

"Now, Mrs. Jones, just what sort of work did your husband do before he quit work to . . . um-haw . . . to take up housekeeping?" asks B. J. Bryan, attorney-at-law, with more than a hint of disgust in his voice as he mentions housekeeping.

"Why, I have to stop and think, it's been such a long time. He was an office manager. He even *supervised* about a hundred people."

"I see. And what was his approximate or specific income?"

"Oh, about twenty-four thousand a year, back when that was worth twice what it is now. Why do you want to know that?"

"My dear Mrs. Jones, we must know how much alimony and child support you may reasonably expect, mustn't we?"

"Oh, sure. I wasn't thinking . . . Say, you can forget that stuff about child support. Let him keep the kids.

I'm going to get everything *else,* but he can keep the kids."

Mr. Bryan's eyebrows shoot up like skyrockets on the Fourth of July. "Um-haw! Now, Mrs. Jones, aside from the well-known fact that children are always better off with their mothers, we have the practical aspects of the courtroom to consider. To be perfectly frank . . . well, judges tend to frown upon mothers who do not want their children. That is to say, it rather puts the mother on the outs with the court right at the start. And, if the mother has been—um-haw—shall we say, in the least indiscreet . . . well, that could rather cut the amount that is awarded, you see."

A long pause. Bryan steeples his fingers, and says, "Now, weren't you just going to tell me how much you adore your children, and how much you really wouldn't want them to go to your husband, who drinks rather heavily?"

"Why, oh, yes. I was. Yes," more firmly, "yes, I was!"

The trap has been set *and* sprung for several days now. Talbot Jones sits in a leather wing chair in the law office of Jergins, Watkins, and Brumley.

Jones and Brumley are going over the case for the fifth time. Brumley is upset, and Jones is slightly past that point.

"But, Mr. Jones," begins Brumley, trying to explain something sensibly to a man who doesn't speak the same language and who quite possibly is mad as a hatter, "it just isn't done. What I've been trying to make you understand, is that the courts simply do not award houses and cars and alimony and children to husbands. It is not customary.

"Now, again, my advice to you is to get out and find a job as quickly as you can. You will need the money both for the court fray and for the support payments you most assuredly will have to make after the battle, as it were."

"And I," yells Jones, leaping to his feet, "I want to

keep my house, and my kids. And I think since *she* talked *me* into quitting my job and letting her 'express herself' by supporting me—so she doesn't have to do housework—well, dammit, I think she should go on working and supporting us.

"Besides. Where will a guy my age get a job after eight years without one?"

Brumley is shaken. "Mr. Jones. That just is *not* the way divorce is done!"

Those are the fictional characters. Again, let me repeat that the persons as well as the names in these chapters are figments of my imagination. Keep these chapters, and the tales they tell, in mind as you read the remainder of the book. Having something to refer to should help you understand how the methods that follow may be applied to actual divorce cases.

In law schools, instructors use the same principle for teaching. They offer a "what if" example of a case, and then demand that law students prepare a defense or pleading in the "case" based upon statutes and court rulings. This is known as the "case method" of teaching.

I am not in any way saying that this book could possibly make you into a lawyer. But the case method has worked to teach law principles for many years, and I think this book may—using the "what if" approach—help you better to understand and recognize some aspects of my new divorce defenses and counterattacks.

Chapter VII

AVANT-GARDE VIEWS

Recent books, newspaper articles, magazine offerings, and even general conversations indicate an awakening of the American public to new approaches to personal rights. For example, an article in the *New York University Law Review* went so far as to say that the present and past performance of American judges in the area of sex discrimination "can be succinctly described as ranging from poor to abominable."[1]

There are changing attitudes in other areas as well. Those attitudes involve such apparently diverse subjects as marriage rates, child bearing and care, the changing role of women in modern society, and runaway wives.

Changes in popular views are important. Without the current trend toward recognition of individualism, men would be bound forever into the iron maiden we call divorce.

It is interesting to note that the best indicators of avant-garde thinking on formerly sensitive subjects— venereal disease, self-examination for breast cancer, extramarital affairs—are found in the higher-quality "women's" magazines, and in newspaper articles which usually are buried in the women's news or family sections. Many of the newspaper articles are contributed by wire services, and are usually fairly well researched; they quote persons or institutions whose credentials and reputations give them the title "expert" in the field under discussion.

The kinds and directions of recent articles indicate two trends of import to the man thinking about divorce difficulties. First, public awareness of statistical trends and changing roles is increasing constantly and with growing rapidity (or at least with more printed notice) today. The second is closely tied to the first, but occurs with less frequency in print: there is an emerging concept of the male as a human being. Generally, when the male appears in a societal-review article, he is treated to the same "laboratory animal" examination of which women have become so shudderingly disparaging. But it may be considered a small victory that he is even mentioned. In some cases he is even recognized as "having feelings too."

The articles should not be overlooked by men simply because they are slanted for a female market and do not dwell upon the humanness of men. Quite the contrary.

Those "women's" articles offer a goldmine of information for the male and his attorney preparing to go into a divorce court. Certainly much of the information cannot possibly be used directly in a divorce hearing. However, some of it can be used for statistical breastwork to show that (a) men are discriminated against in areas such as child custody and even visiting rights; and (b) society apparently is moving into a new age of compassion, recognition of individual rights for all, and utilization of the courts as an instrument of social change.

Naturally, I am not saying that mere statistics are enough to win a fair divorce. However, newspaper and magazine articles can provide helpful statistics, and also information an attorney can use in court to evaluate what a judge or jury might be thinking.

For instance, if a man is attempting to win custody of his child in a divorce case, he and his attorney might wish to cite an article such as the one that was nationally circulated not long ago by a major wire service, datelined San Antonio, Texas.

In one publication, the article was headlined, "Divorced Dads Begin Campaign." It read:

> A group of men declaring the laws and courts of Texas discriminate against divorced men and their children have begun a campaign seeking equal financial responsibility by divorced parents and equal voice in child-raising.
>
> Texas Fathers For Equal Rights leader El Cullum says the group contends domestic relations courts in divorce proceedings grant mothers custody of children out of habit and to the repeated detriment of the children.
>
> "Child support should be for the benefit of the child and not for the punishment of the father," Cullum also says.[2]

The article covers the gamut of discrimination in child custody. It is quotable in a legal brief, even though the clipping itself would be hearsay if offered as evidence.

Although one lone article does not indicate a national trend, it is an arrow directing attention to a movement in one geographical region—a movement that well might become national.

Another wire-service article noted, "The number of marriages in the United States last year took its first drop since 1958 while the divorce rate went up for the twelfth year in a row." The article cited Department of Health, Education, and Welfare figures which showed there were 2,223,000 marriages, or a drop of 2.4 percent, in 1974; on the other hand, there were 970,000 divorces. HEW figures showed there were 57,000 more divorces in 1974 than there were in 1973, compared to a drop in 1974 of 54,000 marriages.[3]

A *New York Times* article of March 1, 1975, noted

not only the increase in divorce and the decrease in marriage, but also statistics showing that the 1974 divorce rate was 135 percent higher than that of 1962—the year preceding the official recognition of an upswing in divorce. To further muddy the water for traditionalists, the article cited figures from the National Center for Health Statistics showing that a decline in child-bearing rates, which had been continuous "over the last five years, slowed and leveled off for the first time in 1974. . . ."[4]

Please note: The slowing and leveling off of the five-year decline in birth rate means that both the numbers of births and the birth rate itself *increased*. To me this shows either an unimaginable callousness or a strong faith in our system of government, when viewed in the same referenced frame with the soaring divorce rate. Either parents have no concern for the children who may be born out of wedlock or torn by a divorce, or the parents believe that our socio-governmental system will somehow change things to make life with a single parent or with divorced parents nondamaging for the children. I prefer the hope that it is faith in our socio-governmental (society does, indeed, affect how we are governed) system.

The figures reflecting the increase in divorce and decrease in marriage speak for themselves. To begin the analysis, let me state that one of the few traditions relating to marriage which has—as far as can be determined at this writing—remained little changed is that of the man asking the woman to marry him.

It seems likely that the desire for self-determination of women is not totally responsible for the marriage decline. Certainly "living together" contributes to the figures. But, my contention is that men are becoming more and more repelled by the idea of getting married simply to be divorced shortly thereafter—being demoted from a full partner to a permanently indentured servant.

U.S. Public Health Service records indicate just how quickly marriages end. Those records show that in 1970 the median length of marriages in the United States (based upon statistics from twenty-two states, which gives a moderately firm base for extrapolation) was a mere 6.7 years.[5]

Common sense tells us that 6.7 years gives a couple just about enough time to acquire a good job and the beginnings of that secure feeling, a house, a car or two, children, a stereo music system and the records and tapes to go with it, books, furniture, and all the other "good life" necessities from pots and pans to a pool table. In those median 6.7 years, a married man undoubtedly meets and talks problems with a divorced man . . . a chilling thought. And, on the other side of the fence, with all the divorced men in our society, the unmarried men have to hide to avoid meeting a veteran of the settlement courts.

What does a single man think of the prospects of the marriage-divorce circuit after such a meeting? Just ask any unattached male (except one in the early stage of a passionate love affair). More than likely, he has considered the danger of divorce in connection with his entertainment of the notion of marriage.

Statistical trends in divorce are not too difficult to obtain. The U.S. Bureau of the Census has interviewers running around nationwide asking questions on all sorts of irritating topics, collecting information such as:

In 1973, there were 68,251,000 households in the United States. Of that number, 2,346,000 were headed by a person who was separated, and 3,971,000 had household heads who were divorced.[6]

The Census Bureau also states there were 155 million adults in the United States in 1973, with females leading at 81 million compared to 74 million males. Separated males totaled 1.5 million and separated females totaled 2.7 million. Divorced males numbered

2.7 million, and divorced females were recorded at 4 million.[7]

The discrepancies in the numbers of separated and divorced men and women indicate a trend that may be on its way out. Look at it this way—there are 1.2 million fewer separated men than there are women, and 1.3 million fewer divorced men than there are women. Why? How can that be?

Now that I've posed the questions, I'll admit that I just don't know. But, of course, I am willing to hazard an educated guess.

On the "separated" imbalance, I believe one should seriously consider the possibility of error in the statistics (not necessarily through the fault of the statisticians). Actually, I believe it well within the realm of probability that pride could keep many men from admitting to being separated. Many men, rather than state the situation so bluntly, will under questioning reluctantly admit only, "Well, she felt she needed some time to herself, see . . ."

Before you pooh-pooh the theory, consider that "hope springs eternal in the human breast." Most men think of a separation (though they may know it is completely irrational) as merely a time for their wives to come to their senses, and pretty soon everything will be all right again. Face it, gentlemen, we are reared from childhood to be reasonable *and* romantic at the same time—an impossible combination.

On the other hand, women tend to fall into two main categories. There are those who rather enjoy the dramatic enlivening of their daily lives by announcing, "Yes, Rudolph and I have separated." But probably more numerous—if women's liberation supporters and space scientists are to be believed—are those women who tend to be more open and matter-of-fact about personal matters. In support of this I offer recollections of a television special some years ago. The name of the program and the network broadcasting it have been forgotten. I do recall, however, that the special dealt with the subject of women as astronauts. Among other embarrassing revelations was what was reported as a scientific consensus that women would have a better chance of getting back to earth alive because they were much more willing than were men to admit that they had problems—whether physical or mechanical or in-flight—even when caused by their own mistakes!

Concerning the 1.3 million fewer divorced men than women, I believe a little of the same "pride interference" may have affected the male statistic. However, I believe in future years we will see that 1973 was a turning-point year. You see, I believe that until 1974, men were unaware that they had any rights in divorce cases other than to shut up, pay up, and remarry for companionship and all those other conveniences which led to the old truism, "You can't live with 'em, and you can't live without 'em." (The truism apparently does not hold true for women in relation to men. See the statistics.)

Yes, I believe that men remarry more often than do women. I feel this will change in the future; but through 1973, at least, it was true.

Men remarry. For 1.3 million remarried men their lives must be like those of oxen yoked up for stump-pulling. They not only must support the new wife, but also must house, clothe, and feed the old one who refuses to attach herself to a new meal ticket. Why should she? There's no rush. She has a nice house, a nice car, and an iron-clad guarantee that she will have an income. Well, think about it! If someone gave you lodging, transportation, and a handsome income for *free,* with the stipulation being that you may not remarry (sexual activity is not limited, however), would you not carefully weigh all the advantages and disadvantages before *choosing* again to take up the burden of sharing household responsibilities for only a portion of the income you had been receiving?

In support of my thesis, I offer comments from an article in the February 1975 issue of *Redbook* magazine. One quotation from the cover-advertised article titled, "The Marriage Boom, A Nationwide Report":

> Curiously, among the most compelling evidence of Americans' faith in the institution of marriage is the growing rate at which divorced people are remarrying. Today four out of every five divorced men and women will marry again.[8]

Avant-garde thinking is emphasized in a section that says:

> In fact, the current reappraisal of marriage accounts for many divorces—but that may not be a calamity in every case. As a family social worker in Tennessee sees it, "Women know now that they can work and live independently. They're no longer going to stay married and be miserable."[9]

Although a breakdown by sex is not given in the "getting remarried" statement, I find it heartening that the article noted many breakups obtain as a result of marriage reappraisal. The statement appearing in a leading women's magazine certainly should lend credence to men's complaints that they are not being treated fairly in divorce actions.

Why should men continue to bear the burdens of child support and alimony—and finding themselves new "homes"—when an article in one of the most popular women's monthlies blithely states as well-known fact the ability of women to "work and live independently"?

Further evidence of changing trends in marriage is cited later in the same article:

With 43 percent of American wives working—most out of economic necessity but many because they want a career—housework is becoming an increasingly shared enterprise.[10]

It does raise a couple of questions, though. For instance, if 43 percent of American wives are working outside the home, why do so many men have to pay support after a divorce? (That is disregarding the alimony question of the decades: Why should a man support a woman who no longer is his wife?) Also, if the women have to work out of economic necessity while married, doesn't that indicate inadequate income from the husband's job? If such is the case, then how in the world can the man be expected to pay alimony, child support, house payments, and rent a room and buy food for himself, too? Well, what *is* the sound of one hand clapping? And what's half of nothing?

That February 1975 issue of *Redbook* is a veritable goldmine of avant-garde thinking. In "The Right to Know Love," it is noted:

What we call "humanity" is nothing more than the capacity to love. Those who are deprived of love and enduring ties in early life have been deprived, in effect, of their human rights.[11]

And—

In our courts today, a few enlightened judges have brought this new knowledge to their decisions on child custody. I am sure it does not help them sleep well at night. For if we understand fully the meaning of loss of love to a young child, the burden on the conscience of the court is a terrible one.[12]

There are many fathers who have limited visiting rights, inconvenient court-set visiting times, and no chance to express love to their children—by court order—who wholeheartedly believe those statements.

And what of the deprivation to the father of the love of his children?

"The Right to Know Love" speaks to that point most eloquently:

> In fairness to the modern judge, his moral burden is a larger one than Solomon's. For the ancients, blood ties were the essence of the human bond. But in our time we have come to know that a child's love for his parents is neither instinctive nor a heritable trait like the color of hair and eyes; it is very largely a love born of love.
>
> The child loves because he or she is loved; the beloved parents may be his natural parents or his foster parents or his adoptive parents. "Instinct" or "blood ties" do not guarantee that a natural mother or father will love the child and therefore be loved in return.[13]

Another indication of changing attitudes in the custody debate was discussed in the same article. In the past, mere shacking-up of a mother with custody often was overlooked by a court, and moral unfitness could be proven only by demonstrating that the mother was a one-night-stand, commonly repeating, trollop. Whereas today:

> In the absence of absolute standards of "moral fitness," each judge is free to judge it according to his own views. Thus a family court judge in New York transferred custody of a seven-year-old girl from her divorced mother to her father on these moral grounds: The mother was known to be "cohabiting" (as the court put it) with a man described by the court as "the paramour."
>
> The judge also cited the "character of the neighborhood" in which the mother was living. The Lower East Side of Manhattan, said the judge, was not "a safe place for a small female child to play." The child's

father, who had remarried, was living in a suburban garden apartment. No other evidence of his superior "fitness" was introduced.[14]

A national wire-service article printed on the women's page of a Colorado newspaper addressed itself to the current thinking in the preventive-medicine area, rather than to the current marriage autopsy trends. Gay Pauley, women's editor for United Press International, researched the aspects of a continuing marriage and wrote, "A marriage contract needs regular renegotiation to prevent the 'I do' from becoming 'I don't.' "[15]

Pauley said that Dr. Wallace Denton, professor of child development and family life at Purdue University, commented that "'without exception' married couples' attitudes, needs and goals change through the years."

Marriage contracts (a term Dr. Denton uses in a different sense than the formal written documents covered later in this book) are an integral part of the gear-meshing that keeps a marriage running smoothly. Denton expressed concern about the "soaring divorce rate," and cited figures, Pauley said, "showing that between 1963 and 1972 inclusive, there was a 'phenomenal' 82 percent increase nationally in divorce. There are several reasons for the increase. Americans expect a great deal out of marriage—'sometimes too much,' he said."

Pauley said Dr. Denton stressed a marriage contract, renegotiated from time to time to keep up with changing aspects of a marriage, offers a couple a better chance of remaining together. That's something to keep in mind if you happen to be one of those men mentioned earlier who are or will be remarrying after a divorce.

Of the contract, Dr. Denton said:

[It] is the conscious or unconscious, spoken or unspoken agreement between a man and a woman that governs ways in which each meets the other's needs.

The article went on to say:

Some couples actually write down the terms. . . . Writing down "can be good," he said, although "it sounds cold and calculating. We need some way to develop self-identity. Of course, it'd be impossible to write in all the contingencies. There's a new one every day."[16]

Those are a capsule view of avant-garde thoughts in the areas of marriage, divorce, and custody. From them, one may extrapolate to fit the parameters of most divorce and marriage situations. The major point, of course, is that society is changing its views of "traditional" marriage and divorce. Some judges are recognizing that society is becoming aware of the rights of persons (male as well as female), and are modifying their rulings accordingly into more constitutional— thus more fair—decrees.

Chapter VIII

THE FACTS

So you'll know what you are up against, this chapter is designed to explain some of the realities of divorce today as it exists in most county courthouses across the country. It tells you what's been going on while you thought you were happily married, and sometimes feeling sorry for or envying old Fred, who just got divorced.

To make this all a little easier to understand, we'll take each of the three cases described earlier. We'll point out just what would happen in your average divorce-court case in your average state to the couples in Chapters IV, V, and VI. In later chapters you will be told how to avoid the tar pits of "modern" divorce cases.

Take the case of the Smiths. The people who were so refined and sophisticated that they arranged the entire divorce in a friendly way—before they even bothered their family attorney.

In the example, they simply went to their old family attorney, told him they wanted to split, and explained how they wanted it done. When he was sure he was going to get paid, he went along with the idea and everything went smooth as glass.

That's great. We're all happy for them. However, even if you and your soon-to-be-ex-wife are all that civilized, you could hit a major snag.

In only a few states are lawyers allowed by law or bar associations to represent both sides in a divorce.[1] Even in those states, lawyers are reluctant to handle both sides for fear of cutting a fellow attorney out of a fee. And, where a lawyer does represent both sides, if a dispute later arises between the husband and wife (for example, as to the terms of property division or custody), the lawyer may not choose up sides. He must withdraw from the entire case, and cease representing either of the parties.

Then, there's no-fault divorce. In no-fault states, the law says that neither party, husband or wife, has to be the cause of the breakup. More about this in the next chapter, which discusses no-fault divorce in greater detail.

In no-fault states, however, it seems to be a common practice to divide the property without regard to fault. The paperwork is usually left up to the quickest attorney (most often the wife's, because she is the one who typically has filed for divorce). The court usually still goes along with the wife and her attorney.

Of course, when the idea was first introduced, it appeared to some that the plan was simply to divide all property equally. Quite fair, in theory.

Except for one thing—or two. What if there is a definite cause for the divorce, and what if (for instance) the husband and wife both work, but she spent all her income on clothes and jewelry for herself—and he paid for the house, the cars, and the furniture?

All of a sudden . . . not so fair. Oh, sure, if no-fault worked out the way it was designed, it would be far better than the old wife-gets-everything way. But in many cases it is not fair and, as the sheriff said to the moonshiner, "It may not be bad whiskey, but it sure ain't legal."

If you're lucky enough to be like the Smiths, and to live in a state that will allow the family lawyer to handle the deal with no muss or fuss, more power to you. Or if you're in a no-fault state and your wife deserves half of everything (or more than half), then rejoice. But if either of those cases were true of you, the odds are you wouldn't be reading this book.

Probably your case is like either the Browns' or the Joneses', rather than the Smiths'. Now, admittedly, those fictional couples are extreme. Maybe the only problem in your marriage is that now you or your wife has decided it just isn't working. Then again, maybe you're a wife-beater.

It does not matter. Whatever the cause of the divorce, you have the right under the law not to be tossed out in the snow.

Take Brown's problem. What happens when he goes into the average divorce court?

What happens is the whole thing generally is decided before he even sees the inside of the courtroom. His wife's lawyer has filed a motion stating what the wife wants, and maybe a brief trying to make all that grasping sound semi-reasonable. Brown's attorney has filed a list of Brown's income, bills, savings accounts, checking accounts, real estate holdings, and anything else of value.

If his lawyer is on the ball, the initial hearing will last a little longer than is customary. It may follow the general lines of the following courtroom exchange, taken practically word for word from the transcript of an áctual divorce case (only the names have been changed):

HUSBAND'S LAWYER: Now, you are claiming attorney's fees from your husband, are you not?

WIFE (ON WITNESS STAND): Yes.

HUSBAND'S LAWYER: You will agree that between husband and wife the duty to support is a mutual duty, is that fair?

WIFE'S LAWYER: Objection, your Honor.

THE JUDGE: Sustained.

HUSBAND'S LAWYER: You will agree that your husband's duty to financially support you is counterbalanced by your duty to support your husband by cooking, cleaning house, doing laundry, providing companionship—

WIFE'S LAWYER: Same objection.

THE JUDGE: Sustained.

HUSBAND'S LAWYER: Have you not failed in your obligation to cook for your husband since the day you walked out?

WIFE'S LAWYER: Objection, your Honor.

THE JUDGE: Sustained.

HUSBAND'S LAWYER: Are you not in fact at this time right now supporting another man by cooking, doing his laundry, cleaning his house?

WIFE'S LAWYER: Objection.

THE JUDGE: Objection is sustained. Don't persist in this any further, Mr. White.

HUSBAND'S LAWYER: Your Honor, I would like to make an offer of proof and would seek to show to the Court that Florence Brown has entered into a de facto marriage with another man, that she is supporting him by doing cooking, housecleaning, laundry for him and not for Mr. Brown, and that by seeking an attorney's fee from Mr. Brown she is seeking to impose upon him the burdens of a marriage relationship without returning the benefits.

THE JUDGE: Let the record show the respondent's offer of proof.

HUSBAND'S LAWYER: I will seek to show that Joseph Jacobs is a de facto husband of the petitioner and that he, not Mr. Brown, is under the duty to pay attorney's fees.

THE JUDGE: How can he be her husband when she is still married to your client?

HUSBAND'S LAWYER: Then I would ask the Court to order her to pay Mr. Brown for his housecleaning, cooking, his meals, and to do his laundry.

THE JUDGE: The Court is going to—well, that—it is impertinent, is what it is, Mr. White. It is impertinent and I don't make any such orders as that.

HUSBAND'S LAWYER: All right. Thank you, your Honor.

Significantly, the court openly admitted that it doesn't "make any such orders as that," directing females to pay for their husbands' housecleaning, cooking, or laundry. Presumably, the court enters such orders only in favor of wives, directing males to pay for their wives' cleaning, cooking, and laundry. The implications of sexual discrimination are too clear to be ignored.

More than likely, though, when the big day arrives, Brown and wife, the two lawyers, and the judge get together, as often as not in the judge's walnut-paneled office. The judge mutters something about having "reviewed the pleadings," and then says if there are no further arguments to be presented he will rule on the matter at hand.

The "no further arguments" is part formality, and a good part threat to Brown's lawyer not to make trouble or the wife might get even more than she's asking (which might take some doing).

Probably the lawyers would smile, trying to look both respectful and fond of the judge, and crisply offer "No, your honor," and "nothing more, judge." Which is the judge's cue to say something like, "Fine." And sign a piece of paper.

Now, the signing might be done then and there, or it might come later; but it will be signed—with or without the lawyers' fight—under the current system. One thing is certain, and that is that the paper will say more than "fine" on it.

It will say quite a bit in nice, official-sounding language. Which boils down to one major thing: Brown already has been illegally barred from his house for a couple of months at least, but *now*, by God, he'd better not get within a mile of it or he'll go to jail—and nobody gives a damn that he can't even visit the place he's making payments on. And he doesn't have to worry about scratching the furniture while he moves it from the house to his second-floor apartment, either. He won't be moving any of that nice furniture. Unless his ex-wife decides to marry her artist, Brown will be so strapped by the alimony, child support, and car and house payments that his new "home" will be furnished in early Salvation Army.

But *she* was the one messing around? Well, traditionally interpreters of the law (judges) seem to have been saying, "My dear sir, any man who can't control his own wife doesn't deserve any legal breaks."

"But," cries Brown, "I was only trying to be liberal and unchauvinistic by letting her go out and have a career!"

The traditional court judgment: "Nonsense! Any fool knows that women can't handle that kind of responsibility. Turn them loose from the kitchen and they're bound to get into trouble. You see, it's all your own fault."

There stands Brown. Well, scratch off one male advocate of women's rights.

His ex-wife gets the child, and Brown gets visiting rights. Every third Tuesday.

Perhaps the only consolation is that *both* the Browns really do care about and for the child. Maybe the kid's emotions will survive his parents' divorce.

In contrast to Mrs. Brown, Mrs. Jones does not love her children. In fact, she can't stand the sight of them. But she gets custody in the traditional court.

What's the deal? Jones is the one who always took care of the kids. He fed them, bathed them, cleaned up the puke when they got the flu, and he made sure they took their vitamins.

"Ahem," the judge clears his throat, mainly to try and cover his embarrassment. "In answer to your question about custody, Mr. Jones, I must point out that you don't even have a job. And, speaking in defense of certain laws concerning—er—eccentricities, we find it rather odd from the masculine viewpoint that you would prefer to do housework instead of being gainfully employed." In other words, he's saying, "Listen, queer, you think I want some eager young lawyer breathing down my neck for handing over two defenseless little boys to a weirdo like you?"

But Talbot Jones doesn't have a job. And he's getting into the age range where people are reluctant to hire a man. How in the world is he supposed to pay the alimony and the child support?

The judge says, "I'm afraid that is not my responsibility. I merely carry out the laws, just as you must abide by the orders of this court." Translation: "Listen, that's the way it's always been done. Besides, maybe a little sweat and suffering will straighten you out!"

Somehow Jones gets the impression the judge thinks just because a man stays home to take care of the kids and the house (because his wife will not do it), well, it sounds like the judge thinks Jones is homosexual. What about those pictures of Jones in bed with "that floozy"? The photos introduced as evidence?

The judge says, "I'm not here today to pass judgment on your sexual proclivities, Mr. Jones." He means, "But, I'm not convinced . . . after all, you do keep house, eh? And, if you show up here on a charge of molesting little boys, it won't surprise me a bit."

However, the judge is not all bad. He gives Jones a whole thirty days to find a job and to make the first support and alimony payments.

It goes pointedly unnoticed by all but Jones that the alimony and support (without the mortgage and car payments) are nearly double what his wife's entire take-home pay was before he suddenly again became the provider. When Jones brings this up, the judge says if he can't meet the payments because the job he'll be getting doesn't pay enough, he'll have two choices.

Jones can find another, higher-paying position, or he can work two jobs. Lowering the alimony and support might be considered, but only after all other measures are exhausted. After all, we can't just fling women and kids onto the welfare rolls, can we? And it is difficult for a mother to work and rear children, isn't it?

Summarizing the typical judicial approach to divorce is really simple. Courts just keep doing it the way it's been done for years—you know, from back in the time when a man beat his wife into submission (often quite legally) or sort of put her away from himself and supported her to show the world he was a gentleman.

Of course, in those old days, a woman out in the world of work was an oddity—or was doing rather private work in a business with other women doing the same "nighttime" job.

Now, we are civilized. Women can be respectable and still hold a job. It is their legal right.[2]

However, it's too bad. Too bad, that is, that a man cannot have use of the same constitutionally guaranteed rights that for years have insured woman's fortune.

You know the law. The one about equality. The one about freedom from involuntary servitude.

Chapter IX

NO FAULT? FOUL!

As you may have gathered by now, I disapprove of no-fault divorce laws (now politely renamed "dissolution of marriage" laws) as they are set up and used.

In the first place, no-fault laws seem to be designed to cover everything, without stating what is covered.

That is, they are too broad and don't explain themselves. I feel no-fault laws are unconstitutional because they are too broad; they try to cover everything with one "ground" for divorce: "irretrievable breakdown" of the marriage.

It sounds real nice, doesn't it? Even at first glance some good lawyers might say, "Well, what's wrong with that?"

What's wrong is best pointed out by the question: "Can you describe irretrievable breakdown of a marriage?"

Go ahead. Fire away at it. I don't care what you come up with.

Because whatever you say, whatever description you offer—is not listed in the law!

The due-process clause of the Fourteenth Amendment to the United States Constitution requires laws to state specifically what conduct will result in your being deprived of life, liberty, or property.

In a recent case, the United States Supreme Court found the words "contemptuous treatment," appearing in the Massachusetts law forbidding desecration of the flag, to be void for vagueness.[1] Certainly the term "irretrievably broken" is every bit as vague as the term "contemptuous treatment."

The Supreme Court has said, "Vague laws in any area suffer a constitutional infirmity."[2]

Parliament in England has enacted a no-fault divorce law, too. But the English version elaborately defines the term "irretrievably broken down." About the definitions that appear in the English version (but which are singularly absent in the American version) Judge Ormrod of the Queen's Bench Division of the High Court of Justice, ruling in the divorce case of *Pheasant* v. *Pheasant,* had this to say:

> The question of irretrievable breakdown has not, therefore, been left at large for the court to determine, no doubt because it was realised that, except in the clearest cases, this is not a justiciable issue. Without guide lines the court has no means of judging what one person, let alone two, may decide to do in the future in relation to their marriage if there is any doubt about it. . . .
> Applying this test to the facts of the present case I have no hesitation in holding that there is nothing in respondent's behaviour which could be regarded as a breach on her part of any of the obligations of the married state or as effectively contributing to the break-up of the marriage. . . . Petition dismissed.[3]

The Family Law Section of the American Bar Association is staunchly against no-fault divorce, particularly because of its use of the term "irretrievably broken" as grounds for dissolving the marriage. The Family Law Section feels that "irretrievably broken" is not definitive enough: every person has his own impression of what makes a breakdown irretrievable—from disliking different breakfast cereals to murderous assaults.

If you put a hundred people in a room and gave each of them a pencil and a piece of paper, and asked them to write down what they think would cause a marriage to be irretrievably broken—you'd get a hundred different answers. And every one of those answers would be specific. Also, of course, they would be based upon some marriage each person knew about.

You would get answers like: "When the husband keeps beating up the wife . . ." or "The wife is a drunk and has set the house on fire six times with the kids in bed . . ." or "The husband and wife haven't spoken to each other for two years, and they get their sex with somebody else."

Those are specific. They give some idea as to why a marriage could pretty well be considered deader than a doornail. Such specifics should be spelled out in the law.

The original idea of no-fault was to eliminate bitterness in divorce by doing away with the necessity of having to formally allege and prove specific acts of misconduct by the defendant. If the proponents of no-fault thought they could eliminate acrimony in an aggravated case merely by decreeing that acrimony should no longer exist, then the proponents of no-fault were incredibly naïve.

Speaking of England's no-fault divorce law, Sir Roger Frey Greenwood Ormrod of the Queen's Bench Family Division, in his opinion in *Pheasant* v. *Pheasant,* observed:

> So far from saving "bitterness, distress and humiliation" it produced a degree of humiliation of the petitioner which is unique in my experience.[4]

As I write this, there are at least twenty-three no-fault states. They are: Alabama, Arizona, California, Colorado, Connecticut, Florida, Georgia, Hawaii, Idaho, Indiana, Iowa, Kentucky, Maine, Michigan,

Missouri, Montana, Nebraska, Nevada, New Hampshire, North Dakota, Oregon, Texas, and Washington.[5] In addition, certain other states have some of the no-fault characteristics. Such states include Delaware, Louisiana, and New York.[6] States constantly revise their statutes; therefore, this list may change in the course of printing this book.

In a no-fault state, all a person has to do is go into the court and say the marriage has suffered an "irretrievable breakdown." That's what the law says the court has to hear, and so the divorce is granted.[7] It's nobody's fault, so nobody's hurt, right?

Nonsense! A man is sitting at home one day and a process server comes to the door and hands him a piece of paper that says he's being divorced because of an "irretrievable breakdown" in his marriage. Then, if the fellow thought he had a pretty good marriage, he sits around for a couple of days trying to figure out what the irretrievable breakdown *is!*

In short, the Fourteenth Amendment says a person must be allowed due process of law, and that includes being told what he is charged with. The objection that the Uniform Dissolution of Marriage Act is void for vagueness is based on this concept. But vagueness is not the only constitutional objection to no-fault divorce.

Article I, Section 10, of the federal Constitution says that "No State shall . . . pass any . . . Law impairing the Obligation of Contracts. . . ." The no-fault laws clearly impair the obligation of marriages contracted prior to their passage. Such laws do more than merely change the remedy afforded for a *breach* of the marriage relationship: they abolish the concept of breach altogether, and substitute an entirely new understanding of the marriage relationship—one the husband never agreed to when he got married.

Going back to the law governing every other type of contract, we find you can't go into court and say,

"Judge, I want out of my contract with Ox Goring Company because of an irretrievable breakdown in our relationship," and expect to get out of your contractual obligations.

The first thing the judge is going to say is, "What do you mean by an irretrievable breakdown in your relationship?" And you'd better have a damn good explanation of what you mean, or you are not going to get out of that contract and you *are* going to end up paying court costs.

As I said earlier, marriage is a contract. It's called a contract all over the place.[8] And we know the states are powerless to pass laws letting people run around breaking contracts without a good reason.

The classic case interpreting the contract clause of the constitution is *Dartmouth College* v. *Woodward*.[9] That case was argued before the Supreme Court by Daniel Webster early in the history of our new nation. It was decided in 1819 by a Court composed of the founding fathers of our American legal heritage. The decision by Chief Justice John Marshall and by Mr. Justice Story—the great Joseph Story—is truly a landmark in American jurisprudence.

Surprisingly, both Marshall and Story discussed the unconstitutionality of no-fault divorce laws—*one hundred and fifty years before enactment of the first no-fault divorce law!*[10] Their comments are every bit as pertinent now as they were a century and a half ago, and are set out at length in the footnotes to this chapter.

The no-fault laws appeal to the worst in mankind: greed. They permit the person at fault to profit from his or her own breach of the marital obligation.

By implication, the laws say that a person no longer is under any obligation to keep his or her marriage vows.

That approach of the law leaves one person in a

marriage—usually the husband—holding the bag and wondering, "What the hell did I do wrong?"

Some legal and societal authorities feel no-fault divorce laws, in effect, encourage trial marriages. The laws create the attitude, some say, of "What the heck! If we don't like it, we can just get out of it, and it isn't any problem. And while we're trying it out, nobody can call us immoral or anything, because we'll be married!" With an incentive to succeed like that, is it any wonder marriages are doomed to fail and the divorce rate skyrockets?

What all this boils down to is that the law should demand a reason, an explanation of why a person wants to have the marriage contract ended by the court.

It's really very simple. It's also really very fair, and constitutionally acceptable.

If a woman (or for that matter, a man) wants out of a marriage, there's a reason. She should tell the court the reason, and that way the husband also knows why she wants out. If the husband disagrees with the wife's idea, then the husband can try to convince her and the court that she's wrong. If both agree to end the marriage, they should be permitted to do so.

That's called due process of law. One side of a dispute being able to defend itself against accusations made by the other side. And against loss of property.

No-fault is like farmer Albatross going to the court and saying that Jimmy Clean stole one of his chickens —and the court sending out the sheriff to take Jimmy off to prison without even hearing what Jimmy has to say about the whole thing.

In Great Britain, way back before the United States was around, that sort of thing used to happen. The English demanded due process of law—or else. The result was that on June 15, 1215, King John signed the Magna Charta (or Great Charter), which guaranteed civil and political liberties to the people.

When we Americans built this nation, we designed a

Constitution that followed the lines of the Magna Charta, but which went even further toward guarantees of liberty. Including due process of law and the sanctity of contracts.

The Uniform Dissolution of Marriage Act tries to go around that constitution. If public confidence in the judiciary is to remain, this must not be tolerated by the courts.

Chapter X

SLAVERY!

The sexism inflicted upon males by the divorce courts of our land is no less dehumanizing than the racism formerly inflicted upon blacks by courts in certain states.

It is illegal to own slaves in the United States of America.[1]

Therefore, it would seem that it is also against the law to force a man to support a woman when the marriage is dead. Especially if the marriage was ended by the woman, and most particularly if the woman killed the marriage by doing something like running around before she filed for divorce.

Your lawyer can and should point out, in state or federal court, that under our laws women now are considered equal to men and just as capable of holding jobs—and of supporting themselves—as men are![2]

Your lawyer will say that making a man support his ex-wife is "peonage," or in less polite language, slavery! Your lawyer also will point out that it is illegal.

In the case of *Plessy* v. *Ferguson*, the United States Supreme Court defined slavery:

Slavery implies involuntary servitude—a state of bondage; the ownership of mankind as a chattel, or at least the control of the labor and services of one man for the benefit of another, and the absence of a legal right to the disposal of his own person, property and services.[3]

Slavery is the forced working for someone else. The law says women are able to work for themselves, and in fact it demands that they be given equal opportunity to work.[4] Here's a chance for your wife to exercise her right.

About that word "peonage." It comes from "peon," which is defined by the courts as a "species of serf, compelled to work for his creditor until his debts are paid."[5] In a divorce case, the debt is never paid.

Your state law says it *is* legal to force a man to support his ex-wife? So what?

Everyone knows that despite repeated attempts (by some Southern states, for example) to prove otherwise, *federal civil rights law carries more weight than state laws!*[6] 42 U.S. Code § 1994 says, "The holding of any person to service or labor under the system known as peonage is abolished and forever prohibited . . . in liquidation of any debt or obligation, or otherwise. . . ."[7]

Your attorney also will point out that the Thirteenth Amendment to the Constitution of the United States says:

> Neither slavery nor involuntary servitude, except as punishment for crime, whereof the party shall have been duly convicted, shall exist within the United States, or any place subject to their jurisdiction.[8]

Your attorney will point out that the only way you can be forced to work involuntarily is if you've been convicted of a crime. Being on the verge of divorce and being actually divorced are not crimes under the laws of man.

Commenting on the Thirteenth Amendment in the case of *Bailey* v. *Alabama,* the Supreme Court said that:

While the immediate concern was with African slavery, the Amendment was not limited to that. It was a charter of universal civil freedom for all persons, of whatever race, color or estate, under the flag.

The words involuntary servitude have a "larger meaning than slavery." . . . The plain intention was to abolish slavery of whatever name and form and all its badges and incidents; to render impossible any state of bondage; to make labor free, by prohibiting that control by which the personal service of one man is disposed of or coerced for another's benefit which is the essence of involuntary servitude.[9]

Your lawyer will admit in his brief that marriage is a contract, but will point out that the law prohibits people from contracting themselves into indenture.[10] It is no answer that you voluntarily entered into the contract of marriage, or that the contract is authorized by state law.[11] It just is not legal to make you work out a "debt" to your ex-wife—not even a contractual debt—especially when that debt is placed upon your head by a judge.

Also, the United States Supreme Court has ruled that it is illegal to put someone in jail or prison for quitting his job,[12] and that no amount of debt is sufficient to allow a court or private person to make the debtor work unwillingly![13]

The mutual obligation of support (and the obligation of support must always be mutual) existing between parent and child may be an exception to this rule.[14] Interestingly, the early federal cases mention the parent-child relationship as an exception to the law prohibiting peonage, but speak of no corresponding exception for the relationship between a spouse and a former spouse.

Children, therefore, put a slightly different light on the scene, but only in the area of child support, which I'll talk about later.

Okay. Say your wife is the one who filed for divorce.

Your lawyer can point out in his memorandum to the federal court that the wife is the one who wants to break the marriage contract.

You may be thinking that all that does is prove your wife's point—that ending the marriage is breaking a contract and you owe her. If that's what you're thinking, forget it. What the marriage-is-a-contract point proves (when your wife files for divorce) is that your *wife* is breaking the contract!

Example:

What happens in business when, say, the Ox Goring Company breaks a contract with Hidebinders, Inc.? Why, Hidebinders sues Ox Goring, of course. And Ox Goring (which broke the contract) pays damages.

In the case of your marriage, if your wife is the one breaking the contract—why should *you* be the one to pay the damages? That just isn't the way things work in all the rest of the law! It is out-and-out discrimination against you, just because you happen to be a man! (Facts and figures documenting the appalling magnitude of this discrimination will be presented in a later chapter in this book.)

When there are no children, there's no legal or moral or constitutional backing for forcing labor (with the threat of imprisonment) on a man to make him support his former wife. Oh, there might have been some reason for pressure from society way back when society also said women should not work outside the home. But, now? In our enlightened age? Hardly.

Examples of cases where no alimony should be given are those of Mrs. Brown and Mrs. Jones. Florence Brown wanted her artist—and to house him in the home poor Mr. Brown sweated to make comfortable. I say, "Let her have her artist, but let her artist find some way of housing her, or let her find some way of housing him—other than in Mr. Brown's home!"

Diane Jones wanted the freedom to work (fine!), and she wanted to run around with other men, and she wanted to torture the hell out of Jones. Talbot Jones agreed to her having a job, and he agreed to take care of the house and kids, and he even tried to ignore her running around for a while. She got what she wanted.

In no-fault divorce states, the woman can be a round-heels, can beat the kids, can be a lush or any number of different things upsetting to different people, and she can file for divorce and get half of everything and alimony too! And she's the one wrecking the marriage in the first place!

Your lawyer can argue that forcing a human being to labor to the profit of another, when a marriage relationship no longer exists between them, and particularly when the relationship was terminated at the option and through the fault of the individual seeking court appointment as taskmaster over the life and fortune of the innocent spouse, constitutes slavery and peonage within the meaning of the constitutional and statutory prohibitions.

Of course, there are the other facets. The man may be a wife-beater, a boozer, or a loser. Or maybe the two people just decide they can't stand the sight of each other anymore. In cases like that, the property should be divided fairly.

If the woman works, she should get those household items she paid for (assuming the man has a job, too), and the man should get those that he paid for. Big things like houses and cars should be divided equally, according to the way the law was *intended*.

If the woman doesn't work, and she wrecked the marriage, she should not get anything.[15] If she doesn't work, and the divorce is merely a parting of the ways, the distribution of property should be equal, with the thought in mind that the man paid for the big things (house, car, boat, trailer) more heavily than he did for the washer and drier.

If you live in a no-fault state, and your nonworking wife wants out of the marriage and you don't have reasons (other than the divorce) to hate her guts, be man (translate to "humane") enough to let her go. If she cleaned your house, cooked your meals, and washed your socks, she earned part of the property you paid for.

Fair is fair. But, after a fair division of property, your obligation ends. She earned some of the things you both owned, but she has no legal hold on anything you earn after the divorce.

After the divorce, she's no longer pulling a share of your joint burden. There is no joint burden anymore.

You're doing your own cooking and laundry, and she's no longer providing companionship (sex, either!). You've split the marriage and the property and the debts. What's yours is yours.

The time has come for our courts to face the constitutional fact that alimony should be no more than, perhaps, an ordinary money judgment not enforceable by imprisonment—and that no alimony should be allowed at all when the marriage has been ended by a person seeking to profit from his or her own breach of the marital contract.

Chapter XI

THE EQUAL RIGHTS AMENDMENT

In this book you are being told that you are being railroaded in your divorce case. You're also being told that the local judge who is doing it is breaking federal law. In 28 U.S. Code § 1343 (3), it says that you can go straight to United States District Court, pay a fifteen-dollar filing fee, and try to get that court to order your local court (and even your state supreme court) to treat you and your wife equally.[1] More about the procedures later.

The why and how are written into the laws of this nation, a nation known throughout the world for its *fair* treatment of the individual. Some courts once might have tried to beg off deciding a sex case based on some of the earlier equal rights laws. They would have said that those laws really were aimed only at racial discrimination or voting rights.

From 1873 until just a few years ago, court rulings refused to interpret the equal-protection clause of the Fourteenth Amendment as applying to sexual discrimination.[2] Then, in 1971, the California Supreme Court said in the case of *Sail'er Inn, Inc.* v. *Kirby:*

> Sex, like race and lineage, is an immutable trait, a status into which the class members are locked by the accident of birth. What differentiates sex from non-suspect statuses, such as intelligence or physical dis-

ability, and aligns it with the recognized suspect classifications is that the characteristic frequently bears no relation to ability to perform or contribute to society.[3]

In 1971, the United States Supreme Court decided the case of *Reed* v. *Reed,*[4] and unanimously struck down an Idaho law that gave preference to males seeking court appointment as administrators of estates.

In 1973, the United States Supreme Court decided the case of *Frontiero* v. *Richardson,*[5] and in a plurality opinion suggested that "classifications based upon sex, like classifications based upon race, alienage, and national origin, are inherently suspect and must therefore be subjected to close judicial scrutiny."[6] The Court struck down a federal law requiring female members of the armed services to prove they were providing more than half the support of a spouse claiming medical and other benefits. Spouses of male members of the armed services were entitled to such services automatically.

Following the enlightened decisions in *Reed* and *Frontiero,* the cause of sexual equality suffered a short setback with the 1974 decision of *Kahn* v. *Shevin.*[7] In that case, the Supreme Court saw nothing wrong with a Florida law granting property tax exemptions to widows but failing to grant equal exemptions to widowers.

But the Supreme Court then agreed to hear an appeal in which the Utah Supreme Court, relying upon the decision in *Kahn* v. *Shevin,* upheld the constitutionality of a state law treating children in divorce cases differently on account of sex.[8] That case, as of this writing, still is undecided by the United States Supreme Court.

However, on January 21, 1975, the Supreme Court struck down a Louisiana law giving women automatic exemption from jury service in criminal cases.[9] But one week later, the Court decided this decision should not be applied retroactively to cases tried before January 21, 1975.[10]

The United States Supreme Court is vacillating.

Speaking of the history of sexual equality, New York attorney Doris L. Sassower says, "The principle of women as legal inferiors eventually became so deeply imbedded in our case law as to defy elimination without amending the Constitution itself."[11]

That which should seem fairly clear under the equal-protection clause of the Fourteenth Amendment will be made even clearer to the courts when the next addition to the Constitution is ratified. The addition to which I refer is the new Equal Rights for Women amendment, more correctly Equal Rights Amendment, or ERA for short. The amendment is viewed by many women's-rights advocates as the one that will set females free, no longer to be "kitchen and bedroom slaves" to men. But, by the nature of our laws, it will free men, too. (Ratification is several states short at this writing, and may not be achieved until late 1976— in time for the Bicentennial.)

Congress sent the Equal Rights Amendment to the state legislatures for ratification on March 22, 1972. If the ERA is ratified by at least the minimum of thirty-eight states required by the Constitution, the ERA will become the Twenty-seventh Amendment to the United States Constitution. At this writing, it appears the proposed amendment will pass despite the fact that some women's groups are joining the opposition.

Interestingly, one of the most oft-heard points of contention among women is the fear that public restrooms will become unisexual (one wonders if that truly is the major fear, or if it actually is just the one most interesting to members of the news media). The female opponents say things like, "Equal, yes. But still different."

The wording of the ERA:

Section 1. Equality of rights under the law shall not be denied or abridged by the United States or by any State on account of sex.

Section 2. The Congress shall have the power to enforce, by appropriate legislation, the provisions of this article.

Section 3. This amendment shall take effect two years after the date of ratification.[12]

Please note that the words "man" and "woman" do not appear anywhere in the text.

In Section 1, the ERA declares that legal rights shall not be abridged "on account of sex." Quite plainly, that would apply to such things as the right not to be a slave (kitchen, bedroom, or alimony), and the right not to be stripped of one's property because one is male—especially without a true trial by one's peers (plural!) determining that one has committed a culpable act.

Section 1 also tells us that current divorce and support and property division laws no longer may be used to deprive a man of his home, his children, or his income, solely because of his sex. The ERA will supersede all other laws in the area, ensuring civil and personal rights.[13]

State laws on the subject are patently discriminatory against males, both in the language of the laws and—even more often—in the judges' application of those laws.

The importance of Section 2 may not become apparent immediately: that section, you see, gives Congress power to enforce the amendment itself.

Why am I ecstatic about yet another chance for the federal government to poke its nose into our business?

Why: The Congress, under Section 2, may say to the states, "Gentlepersons (no sexism, you understand), would you mind explaining your rationale for kicking all those men out of the houses for which they have broken their backs?

"And, perhaps, you might also tell us how you justify putting a man in the chains of legal bondage, as it were?

"With the threat of even more dire consequences if he fails to submit—just to allow a female citizen to live a life of leisure? By the way, hadn't you heard? We freed women, and all slaves . . . several times.

"We (in 1964, for the record) made it a law that women have the right to support themselves with equal pay for equal work."

And then Congress, after listening to the usual stream of totally inapplicable apologia and drivel, might say:

"Hummph. Not good enough. You are violating every right of those men.

"You have made them slaves to women who no longer reciprocate in a domestic arrangement, or any other mutually beneficial compact, and who could get a job just as well as a man if they tried, and could even support the man.

"You have taken away men's property without any consideration at all for the guarantee of due process of the law—and we do not consider your current 'it's always been done that way' logic to live up to constitutional standards.

"Also, with those support payments, you have literally imprisoned men in their circumstances (generally poverty) by circumventing the Constitution again."

Most importantly, under Section 2, Congress might *order the states to change the divorce laws and the ways in which judges traditionally handle divorce cases.*

Moreover, if the states do not listen, Congress could enact a National Divorce Law that conforms to all guarantees of civil and personal rights!

Although it may be years in the making, just such a divorce law will become reality. With inflation, recession, mini-depression, and so forth, as personally crushing as they are economically, there is a more than even chance (I do not advocate, merely predict) that more and more men will hear the amount of alimony they are ordered to pay, and the house and child and car losses on top of that—and will look the judge in the eye and say, "I will not pay it. Send me to jail!"

If a large enough number of men go to jail for refusal to abide by the divorce-court decisions, the burden on taxpayers will become even more oppressive.

We all know what happens then: we taxpayers yell our heads off. We demand change. We vote judges out of office.

What is the most logical way to remedy the problem? Either change the state laws and rulings to comply, or enact a National Divorce Law.

I believe it would be reasonable to make the law retroactive, thus opening the door for personal and class-action suits to recover losses incurred because of the imposition of illegal court renderings.

Congress might be tempted to put in a provision denying suits to recover damages as reparations for injustices of the past. I think such a provision could be fought and beaten . . . but that's another book at a later time.

Section 3 also has possibilities. However, they are of the variety normally overlooked by legislative bodies—possibly because the chase is too exciting to pass up, so the barn door is purposely closed too late in some cases.

Well, who knows? From the way some legislators act (or, more often, don't act), one easily receives the impression they are bored and looking for any way to find some excitement.

My point, of course, is that Section 3 allows a two-year grace period after it is ratified by the required thirty-eight states before the ERA becomes the supreme law of the land. During that time, reasonable states will be getting their houses in order by revising many, many state laws and procedures—including those governing divorce and all it entails.

The Equal Rights Amendment definitely determines what you will be saying in your divorce actions in the various courts.

That's a hint to you and your lawyer to include some of the material on the ERA in your briefs to the courts. Indicate to the courts that you know what your rights are, that you know the direction in which the law is evolving, and that you know the judges are ahead of their time,[14] but you just want to remind them that you know . . .

Chapter XII

SOME TRAILBLAZING

In law, *substance* is—If someone punches you in the mouth, and you didn't provoke him, then you can sue him.

In law, *procedure* is—If someone punches you in the mouth, and you didn't provoke him, there is a method you must use while suing him. The method includes papers needed, motions to file, and when and how to present them.

Thus:

Substance is *what* you can do.

Procedure is *how* you do it.

As just one example, we know that the Fourteenth Amendment prohibits any state from denying to any person within its jurisdiction the equal protection of its laws. That is a substantive right. Several procedures exist for enforcing that right.

Back in 1703, an English judge observed, "It is a vain thing to imagine a right without a remedy; for want of right and want of remedy are reciprocal."[1]

In law schools today, this principle is paraphrased in the maxim "for every right there is a remedy."

Coming soon in this book are more bits of substantive divorce information. That is, I'm going to tell you what you can do in your divorce case.

Also showing on different pages are bits of procedural information for divorce actions. That is, I'm going to tell you how to do the substantive things, the things you *can* do.

Well, as the dentist said after he didn't find any cavity, "That wasn't so bad, was it?"

It wasn't too bad, was it? In just a couple of minutes, you learned what it takes some law students weeks to figure out.

Chapter XIII

WHAT

(Three Ways to Go)

In fighting your divorce, there are three possible ways to go. I especially like two of them.

Why? Because they're the ones I feel offer the best chances of success, naturally.

First, I'll tell you the one way you should avoid like having a radio transmitter on in a dynamiting area. That is the state-court appeal route.

The major reason to stay away from the state appeal system is that if you go that route—you have just legally kissed your right to appear in federal court goodbye![1] You just don't want to do that, because a federal court has more direct relation to the main issues you'll be urging. That is, you will be attacking the state divorce laws on the grounds they are repugnant to the United States Constitution.

The only time you go into the state higher court system is if the federal district court directs you to do so.[2]

The other two ways of attacking your problem:

1. A request to empanel a three-judge federal court to enjoin your state divorce-court judge from violating your rights. This is a separate suit in the United States

District Court filed against your local judge as defendant.

2. A removal of the divorce suit itself to federal court based on 28 U.S. Code § 1441 (federal question) or on 28 U.S. Code § 1443 (civil rights), or even better on both sections. This technique actually transfers the divorce suit to the United States District Court from the state court in which it originally was filed.

The three-judge suit and the removal device are alternative procedures. Either can be accomplished more economically than an appeal within the state appellate system, since the filing fee in federal court is only fifteen dollars and since an expensive transcript of the divorce trial in state court is unnecessary because the trial has not yet even taken place.

To come out on top of your divorce suit, you will have to get your lawyer to jiggle some memories. You may (through your attorney) completely upset the judge who is to hear your case.

You see, you are either going to remove your case from your local court to the United States District Court, or you are going to sue your local judge in federal court.

Oh, yes you can! I did it!

It is not something you do every morning. But it is your right. Written on a piece of paper stored under glass in an eastern city are guarantees of legal rights— including something about "redress of grievances."[3]

Now, federal court is not the place to try every single divorce case.

Those majestic courts should be for big things involving lots of people, right?

Sure. The fact remains that the federal court is the ideal place in which to set a precedent. That precedent should push state courts into giving men equal justice in divorce cases. Then we wouldn't have to worry about getting screwed in local divorce courts.

Let's get closer to home. One you'd like to keep. If

you want to come through *your* divorce with part of
your hide still attached, you'd better consider going to
federal court. If you don't, your local friendly judge
may pat you on the back and send you out into the
cold—looking and feeling like a too-closely sheared
sheep.

Get that through your head. It is a fact of your life,
now.

One point here: To *remove* your divorce case to federal court on the grounds that you can't get a fair trial
in the state courts (as distinguished from a separate
suit in federal court against your local divorce judge),
you've got to be quick. You have to file in federal
court within thirty days after your wife tells you officially that she wants out.[4]

At the worst, the federal-court move may gain you
nothing more than a stall for time. But in that "stall"
you win a little bit. Sometimes it takes months for the
federal court to get to your case.

Now, pay attention: *During that time, if you have
not already been ordered to pay support, you can
never be charged for anything like "back alimony."*[5]

Actually, the removal to federal court is simpler
than it sounds.[6] But you've got to have one of those
lawyers Talbot Jones was looking for—one with guts
and smarts.

Most law-firm attorneys will just say, "Oh, no.
That's impossible." You'll notice they don't even pick
up a law book to make a good show. Why? Because it's
going to make the local judge mad as hell, and because that lawyer is going to have to go into the law
library and do some research to see how to do it. He's
successful! Why should he have to mess around with
research? Let's just do the divorce the way we do them
all, is his philosophy. Pretend to put up a feeble fight,
sit back, and collect a fat old fee. All the while putting
in maybe three hours (including the court hearing).

Now, if you get one of those "young wise guy know-it-alls just out of law school and still wet behind the ears," it might be dramatically different. He'll look at you across his second-hand desk in his puny hole-in-the-wall office, and say, "Hell, man, I don't know if you can do that! I'll have to borrow the law library at the courthouse and let you know in a couple of days."

And he'll probably be so excited by the idea that he'll go to the law library and forget to eat for two days while he tries to find out if it really can be done—and when he comes out, he'll tell you that this book is right. And can he borrow it for building your case.

Mainly, in either of the two approaches to federal court, you've got to convince the federal court in your area that it has jurisdiction in the case.

However, with just a little bit of legal and statistical research, your lawyer can probably do it.

The research will include statistical information showing that your state courts do discriminate against men in divorce cases.[6] That is why you cannot get a fair trial in your local state court, and that is why the federal court has jurisdiction.

Chapter XIV

HOW

(The Three-Judge-Suit Route)

The ERA will not be the only federal issue you can raise if you decide to go the three-judge-suit route. At present, you can argue that the divorce laws, as applied in your state, violate the equal-protection clause of the Fourteenth Amendment. You might argue that the no-fault concept is unconstitutional. And you might suggest that the application of your state's alimony laws constitutes slavery and peonage in violation of the Constitution and laws of the United States.

A three-judge suit is the soundest approach from the jurisdictional viewpoint. It has the least to offer short-term—but it has the best long-term possibilities. Three-judge suits frequently are used by civil rights lawyers.

In a 3-J (three-judge) complaint, you seek an immediate injunction restraining the state divorce judge from enforcing your state's divorce laws on the ground that those laws are repugnant to the federal Constitution.[1]

With your complaint, you file a "motion to convene a three-judge court."[2]

The single federal district judge who first gets the case then reviews the complaint and motion to deter-

mine if the case is one required to be heard by a three-judge panel.[3] It is.[4] He then contacts the Chief Judge of the United States Court of Appeals, who will appoint two other federal judges to complete the panel. One of the three judges must be from the Court of Appeals.[5]

By the way, an appeal from a properly convened three-judge court goes directly to the United States Supreme Court, bypassing the Court of Appeals entirely![6]

Probably the first thing a federal 3-J court will want to know is, "Do we have jurisdiction if state court remedies have not been exhausted, or if action still is pending in state courts?"

The answer is, yes.[7] This is plainly stated (plain to lawyers, anyway) in the Civil Rights Act of 1871. Your lawyer, of course, will refer to this act in his complaint.

The act says:

> Every person who, under color of any statute, ordinance, regulation, custom, or usage, of any State or Territory, subjects, or causes to be subjected, any citizen of the United States or other person within the jurisdiction thereof to the deprivation of any rights, privileges, or immunities secured by the Constitution and laws, shall be liable to the party injured in an action at law, suit in equity, or other proper proceeding for redress.[8]

The nice thing about this section of the law is that it not only explains why the federal court has jurisdiction no matter what the state court has done on your divorce, but it also comes right out and tells the three judges that the state court judge, the governor, and the state attorney general can't treat you the way they have treated men in past divorce cases.[9]

At any stage in the divorce action, you can file a suit of your own against the state court judge who is presiding over your divorce. You can file the suit in United

States District Court and you can ask that court to keep the judge from ordering you to do anything under state law.

You're suing the judge on the basis that the divorce statute (law) is unconstitutional.

Point *this* out to your lawyer: The law doesn't have to look unconstitutional to be unconstitutional. When the lawmakers wrote it, they may have meant for the law to be fair and equal.

But, if the law has not been *administered* fairly and equally to both men and women, then it is unconstitutional.[10]

Points for your lawyer to make:

1. If a state law isn't administered equally to all, then it is unconstitutional.[11]

2. When you have a state law that is unconstitutional, you don't have to go through all of the state courts before you file in federal court.[12]

3. The usual judicial immunity (he can't be touched) just doesn't protect the judge from being sued in federal court if you have any reason to fear that he is going to take away your constitutionally guaranteed rights.[13]

4. Sexual discrimination is not the only available issue in a three-judge suit; this particular jurisdictional mode may be used to raise almost any federal constitutional objection to any state statute of statewide application (and your state's divorce law is such a statute).[14]

Some of this was mentioned before. This time, your attorney should be making notes, because the footnotes will tell him how to file the suit. The complaint should state that federal jurisdiction is based on 28 U.S. Code §§ 1343(3), 2201, 2202, 2281, 2283, 2284, and 42 U.S. Code § 1983.

Remember, if the divorce law isn't discriminatory in the way it's written, then your attorney should be sure to charge that it *has been made discriminatory* by the way it is used in the state![15]

In your suit, you should ask for a declaratory judgment (you want the federal court to say you have a point). You also should ask for preliminary and permanent injunctions (an injunction is an order telling somebody to stop doing something) to keep the state judge (the one handling your divorce) from depriving you of your marriage, children, and property under an unconstitutional divorce law. And, as I said before, your lawyer should ask for that three-judge court.

Do not try your theories on the state court first! There's nothing that tells you how long you have to file the federal suit, but if you go to state court with the federal issues (unconstitutionality) then the law *does* say that you can't go from there to federal district court.[16]

The way to proceed with this federal court action is to tell the state court (the divorce judge) that you reserve the right to have a federal court decide some federal questions you have. A good way to handle it is to tell the state court at the same time that you file in federal court.

The divorce court judge might be curious about what makes you think you can do all that. Your lawyer can point him to the decision of the United States Supreme Court in the case of *England* v. *Louisiana State Board of Medical Examiners.*[17] In that case, a group of chiropractors were suing to obtain licenses to practice their profession in Louisiana. They filed their suit in federal court against the state medical licensing authority. The federal court directed the chiropractors to sue in the state courts. The chiropractors then brought suit in the state courts, which they lost. Upon their return to federal court, the United States District Court for the Eastern District of Louisiana dismissed their suit, saying that the matter had been decided by the state courts. The United States Supreme Court reversed,

holding that no person may be deprived of his right to
elect to have federal questions decided by the federal
courts. (In the absence of such an election, a state
court may proceed to decide federal issues.) The high
Court talked about the situation of the defendant who
is sued in state court but who has federal defenses he
prefers to raise in the federal courts. He may "reserve" those questions for determination in federal
court, said the Supreme Court.

Once you've made your reservation in state court of
your right to raise your federal questions in federal
court, and once you've filed your suit in federal court,
you can argue in state court that the mere pendency of
proceedings in federal court automatically divests the
state court of jurisdiction to bind the parties.[18] The
case in point is *United Services Life Insurance Co.* v.
Delaney.[19] There, the Texas Supreme Court held that
even where the federal court refused to rule and sent
the case back to the state courts, the state courts still
could not proceed!

You might ask the state court to stay all proceedings
in your divorce until after the federal court has spoken.
Since under the ruling in the *England* case the state
court may not bind the parties until after the federal
case has been adjudicated to final judgment, not even an
express directive from the federal court can operate to
reinvest the state court with jurisdiction!

The people you're suing are: the judge, of course;
the governor; the state attorney general (top lawyer
for the state); and your wife.

We know why you're suing the local judge.

You are suing the governor because he's the gentleman at the top.[20] He's supposed to know what's going
on (although he probably never thought about divorce
as being fair or unfair—he just figured it was a way to
make good money before he became governor). He's
named, too, because the rules for getting a 3-J panel
together on a constitutional case say you must give the

governor and state attorney general "notice" of the hearing.[21]

Then there's the attorney general.[22] When you get right down to it, he's kind of like a shop foreman at a garage.

His job is to see that everything is done by the book. That everything is legal and that it runs smoothly.

When you file your suit, suddenly . . . things are not running smoothly.

Let's see now—who are we forgetting? Oh, yes! Wife! Of course.

Why are you suing your wife?

Two reasons: (1) it gives her attorney something to do besides count the money he thought he was going to get so easily; and (2) mainly because she is the person directly responsible for the courts trying to take away your rights.

Your attorney will file a memorandum of law on the constitutional issues. All this means is your lawyer will write a brief telling the federal court why it should rule on your case. (That is what we were talking about above.)

In the memorandum, your lawyer will point out specifics about your case and how it relates to other, similar cases. He probably will be telling the federal judges what they already know, but possibly haven't thought of yet. That is, that a man in a divorce case hasn't got a snowball's chance in hell of even breaking even on a divorce hearing on the local level—the "tradition" of forgetting male civil rights is too well dug in.

Your attorney will cite statistics like those coming up in Chapter XVI. In equal-employment-opportunity cases and jury-selection cases, the federal courts have held that a statistical showing of sexual imbalance is prima facie proof of discrimination.[23]

Your attorney will point out in legal terms that under United States law women now are considered

equal to men and therefore are just as capable of holding jobs as men are[24]—and that includes the ability
to support themselves and their ex-husbands! (Don't
forget the ERA.)

Your lawyer can point to the Fourteenth Amendment
and the 1973 case of *Frontiero* v. *Richardson*,[25] in
which the U.S. Supreme Court suggested that classifications (like breadwinner or housekeeper) based on a
person's sex are something that should be looked at
closely by the courts. Just like classifications based on
race.

One federal court in Wisconsin already has ques-
tioned the practice of issuing *ex parte* (without the
knowledge of one of the people involved) restraining
orders in divorce cases—where such orders usually
are issued only against men.[26]

And in New York, Judge Sybil Hart Kooper of the
Family Court has ruled that there is something wrong
with the idea that only the mother should be given
custody of children of tender years. In fact, the judge
said that idea violates both New York law and, more
importantly for persons outside New York, the equal-
protection clause of the Fourteenth Amendment to
the United States Constitution.[27]

An equally (I like that word!) interesting ruling
came from the Pennsylvania Supreme Court in 1974.
That state high court knocked out the idea that the
father has the main responsibility for providing support
of children.

The Pennsylvania court said in *Conway* v. *Dana:*

We hold that insofar as these [older] decisions suggest a presumption that the father, solely because of
his sex and without regard to the actual circumstances
of the parties, must accept the principal burden of
financial support of minor children, they may no
longer be followed. Such a presumption is clearly a
vestige of the past and incompatible with the present
recognition of equality of the sexes. The law must not

be reluctant to remain abreast with the developments of society and should unhesitatingly discard former doctrines that embody concepts that have since been discredited.[28]

Once you've got your case going, don't forget to have your lawyer offer to settle out of court. He can quite openly inform your wife's attorney what's in store.[29] Then, after some red tape, when her lawyer is tired, perhaps repeat the offer to negotiate a "reasonable settlement." After a few rounds in higher courts, the attorney realizes he has a tiger by the tail, and grease on his hands. This method has been known to work.

Your fortress is the federal courthouse. Your armaments are the civil rights laws. You have the Constitution and power of the United States of America behind you. You are negotiating from a position of tremendous strength. You are in no hurry; it's your wife who's itching to be single once more. Time is your natural friend and your wife's worst enemy. So you work a trade: you let her get a divorce sometime this decade,[30] and in return she lets you keep your property. A settlement in this situation can be much better for you than one negotiated in the high-pressure halls of your county courthouse: *this* settlement can save you time and money, and probably anything you paid for and want to keep . . . or almost anything.

Chapter XV

MORE HOW

(The Removal Route)

In this chapter I'm going to write about such things as removing your divorce suit from local state court to federal court. This is the second approach I mentioned earlier.

First of all, your attorney should know that this is the one that has to be filed within thirty days after you receive your first notice that you are being sued for divorce—"the initial pleading setting forth the claim for relief" upon which your bid for removal is based.[1]

The three-judge-panel route is actually more solid—less likely to be dismissed from federal court, but slower and not as likely to give immediate relief in your problem.

Although on thinner jurisdictional ice, the procedure of removing the divorce suit itself from state to federal court does have some pretty good points.

One example is a Colorado case, *Patterson* v. *Patterson*,[2] in which the husband was sued for dissolution of marriage. In that case, Mr. Patterson told the judge in advance that he was represented by an attorney and that he wanted a day in court and an opportunity to tell his side of the story.

However, instead of a day in court, my client got an *ex parte* restraining order from the court telling him to move out of his house and commanding him not to talk to his four kids. No hearing. Just the court's order.

At the time of this writing, there are only three officially reported cases in the entire nation dealing forthrightly with sex discrimination in divorce. They are:

1. *State ex rel. Watts* v. *Watts*,[3] decided in 1973 by Judge Sybil Hart Kooper of New York's Family Court, a state trial court. The case holds that it is unconstitutional for courts to favor the mother in awarding custody of children.

2. *Conway* v. *Dana*,[4] decided in 1974 by the Pennsylvania Supreme Court, a state court of last resort. The case holds that the support of children now is the equal responsibility of both parents, and both must be required to discharge the obligation to the best of their respective abilities.

3. *Patterson* v. *Patterson*,[5] decided in 1974 by the United States District Court for the District of Colorado, a federal trial court.

Mr. Patterson took his case to federal court by the removal route under 28 U.S. Code § 1443. In his removal petition, we alleged that he was denied and could not enforce in the state courts of Colorado his equal civil rights as a citizen of the United States. The Colorado statute and the common law of Colorado, we said, show preference toward women in the division of property, awarding of temporary and permanent alimony, in child support and custody, and in attorney fees. In that way, we charged, males are deprived of the equal protection of the laws and of equal civil rights.

The removal was accomplished by filing in federal court: (a) a sworn petition for removal, setting forth the grounds for removal; (b) a removal bond; (c) copies of all state court process, pleadings, and orders; and (d) a certificate of notice and filing, certifying to the federal court that a notice of filing (together with copies of the petition for removal and removal bond) were filed in state court.[6] The removal was completed upon filing in state court: (e) a notice of filing of the petition for removal, with (f) copies of the petition for removal and removal bond attached.

The costs bond, a piece of paper guaranteeing court costs up to five hundred dollars, was obtained from a bonding company for a premium of about twenty dollars.

One of the nice things about the removal method is that *no judge has to act on the removal petition for it to be effective.* All you have to do is file the necessary documents, and the state court's hands are tied automatically.

The law says:

> Promptly after the filing of such petition and bond the defendant or defendants shall give written notice thereof to all adverse parties and shall file a copy of the petition with the clerk of such State court, *which shall effect the removal and the State court shall proceed no further unless and until the case is remanded.*[7] [Emphasis added.]

What that means is that as soon as you file the request to remove the suit from state court to federal court, it is removed!

Even if the federal court later decides that you didn't have enough reason to try to remove your case, it is reversible error for the state court to proceed until the case is returned to that state court.[8] "Reversible error" means that if the state court takes any action on your divorce while the case is in the hands of the federal district court, the state judge who took the action did a no-no.

I'm sure you remember that earlier I mentioned something about a method which could at the very worst save you a little support money. Well, this is the place. A federal court removal.

The way it works is probably plain to you. *If* you ask for the removal *before* the state court judge gives your wife temporary custody of the kids, and before he orders you to get out of your house (by a restraining order), and before the judge orders you to pay temporary alimony and support, then according to law, the judge in your local court cannot do any of those things![9]

Well, let me qualify that. He can do it, but he's not supposed to even think about it until the federal court gives the case back to him—if it ever does.

Some judges are stubborn, and some think they are God. Some might go ahead with things like restraining orders and ordering you to pay alimony, and might disregard the notice from your lawyer telling the judge the case has been removed to federal court.

I believe that if a judge ever did that, he would be acting without jurisdiction.[10] I also believe the judge would be opening himself to possible liability for money damages. You might be able to sue the judge for reimbursement of any money you paid in alimony, for any money you spent to rent a room after he kicked you out of your house, and for money to partially repay you for the inconvenience, embarrassment, humiliation, and mental distress he caused by issuing the orders he did issue. A federal court in Ohio has held that the doctrine of judicial immunity does not insulate a state judge from being sued in federal court for money damages for having acted without jurisdiction.[11]

In a removal to federal court like the one we've been talking about, your lawyer will tell the federal court that you are a person who is denied or who can't enforce his equal civil rights as a citizen of the United States in the courts of the state you live in.[12]

Your lawyer should always keep in mind, and in the court's mind, that the equal-protection clause of the

Fourteenth Amendment is a "law providing for the equal civil rights of citizens."[13] The *Frontiero* case we mentioned earlier[14] now is a part of the equal-protection clause.[15] The Supreme Court has said, "The term 'law' in our jurisprudence usually includes the rules of court decisions as well as legislative acts."[16]

Likewise, the ERA soon may be another "law" providing for the equal civil rights of citizens.

When you go for removal, you should demand an "evidentiary hearing" on your charges.[17] All that means is that you are asking the federal court to listen to evidence why you think you won't be treated fairly in state court. Expert testimony of sympathetic lawyers might be one way to prove sex discrimination. And of course your lawyer should not overlook every opportunity to quote to the federal court from officially reported decisions of the state courts in which a discriminatory attitude is reflected.

At the same time, your lawyer should begin what is called "discovery" to obtain evidence of sexual discrimination. In the discovery part of the case, your lawyer asks the court to order your wife, your local state court, perhaps the attorney general of your state, and your state's judicial administrator to provide you with any and all information you think is needed in your case.

What you want are details of all the divorces in your state for at least the last year, and even better, for the last three or four years—statistics like the ones coming up in the next chapter.

The statistical imbalance between the sexes that is bound to appear is legal proof of sex discrimination.[18]

You also ask the court to order the local judge and your wife to provide you with any other information you feel applies to the divorce. The reason for this is so you will have an accurate picture of what has been done and what is going on.

Of course, if you get a copy, it stands to reason to be sure the federal court gets a copy. That keeps things on the up-and-up. Everybody knows what everyone else has done and is doing. It lets the court know that you plan to do everything in your power to make sure that all the facts are presented.

What does it look like to the federal court when you demand that everything about your divorce and all past divorces in the state be put out in the open?

It looks like you don't have anything to hide, and that you at least suspect that somebody else should be ashamed of something.

By the way, in case your lawyer is trying to remember another way of saying discovery, what he's looking for are "interrogatories," "requests for production," and "depositions on written interrogatories." In the requests for production, your lawyer will ask that the other side produce accurate copies of all laws in the state that apply.

(Of course, pretrial discovery under the Federal Rules of Civil Procedure is not limited to cases *removed* to federal court; this discovery is equally available if you opt in favor of the three-judge-suit route discussed in Chapter XIV.)

At the same time, your lawyer will make "requests for admission." These are specific and sharp as prickly-pear cactus on a bare foot. They ask the other side to admit the things upon which you base your case.

One of the nice things about requests for admission is that *silence from the other side is taken as an admission that you are right!*[19]

Example: Your wife is requested to admit that your state courts show a preference toward women in granting restraining orders against men (and thus kicking them out in the street); in dividing marital property (most property goes to women); in giving permanent maintenance (alimony); in awarding custody of children; in giving the family home; and in awarding attorney fees in divorce cases.

Last but not least, in the requests for admission, your lawyer requests that it be admitted that your local judge shows a decided preference toward women in dividing the property of a marriage.

Something we don't want to forget is that while your attorney is doing all this filing, he will want to file a motion to dissolve any restraining order the state court may have issued before removal.

In a 1974 case, *Granny Goose Foods, Inc.* v. *Brotherhood of Teamsters,*[20] the United States Supreme Court ruled that *ex parte* restraining orders must be dissolved within ten days following removal of the case in which the restraining order was issued.

The high Court's ruling was based on the Federal Rules of Civil Procedure, rule 65(b) of which states that a restraining order issued *ex parte* (that is, without a hearing) expires in ten days except under the most unusual circumstances.

The Supreme Court reasoned that when a state case is removed to federal court, the Federal Rules of Civil Procedure govern that case, even as to orders issued by the state court before removal.

However, where a hearing was held in state court before the order was issued (as is usually the case for temporary maintenance and temporary custody), then the order is not *ex parte.* If there has been a hearing in state court before removal, any orders arising out of that hearing remain in effect after removal of the case to federal court. This is why you will want to remove your case quickly, before the state court has a chance to hold hearings on custody and support and the like.

But even orders issued after a hearing in state court are subject to your right to attempt to have them set aside by the federal court. If the court grants your motion, you are in great shape. You stay home for at least a while longer and don't pay support for sure. At least for a while.

Of course, removal of the case doesn't end the divorce suit. It merely transfers it to the United States Courthouse. Your lawyer also should file a motion to dismiss the suit.[21]

All issues that could have been raised in state court (including other federal issues) may be raised on removal by following the procedure for raising the issues in federal court.[22] But any other federal questions are not *grounds* for removal under § 1443—they are just matters before the court once the case has been removed.

You remember Mr. Patterson? Well, after his case was removed to federal court, he filed a motion to vacate (dissolve) the temporary restraining order that had been issued by the state court.

In his motion, he alleged: (1) that the order violated due process of law by taking away his property without a hearing[23]; (2) that, by prohibiting him from communicating with his children, the order was a prior restraint on the exercise of his right to free speech as guaranteed by the First Amendment[24]; and (3) that in any case, a state court *ex parte* restraining order *must* be dissolved within ten days after the case is removed to federal court.[25]

Mrs. Patterson admitted that the court should grant her husband's motion, and the federal court entered an order vacating and setting aside the temporary restraining order that had been entered by the state court.

In the end, the United States District Court did give the case back to state court. However, in doing so, U.S. District Judge Richard P. Matsch handed down a far-reaching decision. The text of his ruling follows:

MEMORANDUM OPINION AND
ORDER OF REMAND

MATSCH, Judge

L. David Patterson is the respondent in a proceeding initiated by his wife in the District Court in and for the County of Fremont, State of Colorado for the dissolution of his marriage under the applicable Colorado statute providing for such an action upon the basis of a showing that a marriage is irretrievably broken. He removed that litigation to this Court under 28 U.S.C. 1443 alleging that he is denied and cannot enforce in the courts of the State of Colorado his equal civil rights as a citizen of the United States because the Colorado statute and the common law of Colorado prefer females in the division of property, award of temporary maintenance, permanent maintenance, child support, custody and attorney's fees in such cases, thereby depriving males of the equal protection of the laws and equal civil rights. . . .

Counsel for Mr. Patterson has eloquently opposed remand in his brief and he has urged an opportunity to present evidence to support the contention that males are unable to obtain equal rights with females in dissolution of marriage proceedings in the courts of Colorado. There is an offer of proof of a statistical disparity in the award of custody in all such cases during 1972 to create a presumption of sexual discrimination, and a request for admissions of a number of facts tending to support discriminatory treatment of men has not been answered in this case. Additionally counsel for Mr. Patterson cites several Colorado cases in which a discriminatory attitude is reflected. These cases, however, are interpretations of Colorado law before the enactment of the statute under which the present proceeding was brought.

If this Court retains jurisdiction in this matter, consideration must be given to the motion to dismiss the dissolution of marriage proceeding filed herein. That motion raises a venue question and it also contends that the Colorado statute violates the due process clause of the Fourteenth Amendment as being vague and uncertain and it is also argued that it is a law which impairs the obligation of contracts contrary to the prohibition in Article I Sec. 10 of the U. S. Constitution.

Because I am compelled to conclude that 28 U.S.C. 1443 does not permit removal of this dissolution of marriage proceeding, these substantive questions will not be considered at this time. The authorities cited above [citations omitted] restrict the application of this removal statute to cases of unequal enforcement or denial of civil rights on the basis of race. That result is mandated by an historical interpretation of the statute, even though the legislative language is not so restrictive.

It is urged that these cases were determined before the decision in *Frontiero* v. *Richardson*, 411 U.S. 677 (1973). While that opinion is suggestive of the development of sex as a suspect classification within the requirement of a close judicial scrutiny on the question of equal protection, it does not alter or affect the statutory standard for removal of actions from state courts.

Under the authorities cited, it is not only required that one removing an action under 28 U.S.C. 1443 show that he has a right under a law providing for equal civil rights, it must also appear that he is denied or he cannot enforce that right in the state courts. Before removal can be approved in the present case, this Court must find that the District Court in Fremont County will discriminate against Mr. Patterson because he is male. That I am not prepared to do. While the issuance of the *ex parte* temporary restraining order here seems inappropriate to the circumstances and while the statistical offering is disturbing, there is no adequate basis for assuming that the Court in Fremont County will be insensitive to the developments of the law reflected in such cases as *Frontiero* and to the changing economic and social conditions involving the marital relationship.

A remand of this case at this time on a purely procedural basis without a determination of the substantial questions presented by the motion to dismiss will not preclude the possibility of a later look at these questions in a federal court in a different jurisdictional mode.

Upon the foregoing it is

ORDERED that this proceeding is remanded to the District Court in and for Fremont County, Colorado.

Dated at Denver, Colorado, this 19th day of August, 1974.

> BY THE COURT:
> Richard P. Matsch, Judge
> United States District Court

Not meaning any disrespect—rather, applauding—to the brilliant federal judge who issued the decision, it appears to me that he possibly was warning the state courts that divorce cases should be handled more equally in the future. Based of course on "developments of the law," and upon "the changing economic and social conditions involving the marital relationship."

At any rate, Mr. Patterson took an appeal to the United States Court of Appeals for the Tenth Circuit.[26] Because the case was appealed, the federal district court held back on returning the divorce case to the local court (in legal terms, the federal court "stayed its order of remand").

In such a case, until such time as the United States Court of Appeals reviews the case, someone in Mr. Patterson's situation cannot be subjected to discriminatory treatment in the form of orders commanding him to support his wife and children or move out of his house.[27]

Something you should know is that before the *Frontiero* case, and before the ERA, decisions on § 1443 removals limited that kind of removal to cases involving racial discrimination.[28] But there is nothing in the language of the law limiting it to race. The law says:

Any of the following civil actions or criminal prose-cutions, commenced in a State court may be removed by the defendant to the district court of the United States for the district and division embracing the place wherein it is pending:

(1) Against any person who is denied or cannot enforce in the courts of such State a right under any law providing for the equal civil rights of citizens of the United States, or of all persons within the jurisdiction thereof;

(2) For any act under color of authority derived from any law providing for equal rights, or for refusing to do any act on the ground that it would be inconsistent with such law.[29]

Section 1443 definitely needs to be reevaluated in the new light of dawning sexual equality. The Fourteenth Amendment now has been expanded to reach sexual equality. Concerning the expansivity of the Fourteenth Amendment, the Supreme Court has said:

[T]he Equal Protection Clause is not shackled to the political theory of a particular era. In determining what lines are unconstitutionally discriminatory, we have never been confined to historic notions of equality, any more than we have restricted due process to a fixed catalogue of what was at a given time deemed to be the limits of fundamental rights.[30]

With the expansion of the equal protection clause to encompass sexual discrimination, the interpretation to be given 28 U.S. Code § 1443 likewise should be broadened to include all forms of discrimination based upon immutable traits of status into which the class members are locked by the accident of birth.[31]

An "immutable trait" interpretation of the removal law in no way does violence to the statutory language, and in no wise is inconsistent with the pre-*Frontiero* decisions limiting the statute to the only form of discrimination prohibited at the time—race.

Just as the Fourteenth Amendment is being expanded to keep pace with the times, so should § 1443 be expanded to keep pace with the equal-protection clause of the Fourteenth Amendment.

Section 1443 served well in eliminating the racial injustices of the 1960s; it should be permitted to serve equally well in eliminating the sexual injustices of the 1970s. The real question is whether the federal courts will deal as courageously and forthrightly with sexual injustices as they did with the even more difficult and distasteful injustices presented a decade ago by the blacks who first paved the way down Route 1443.

In removal proceedings, the burden is on the state court plaintiff to show that the case should be remanded to the state courts. Thus, any uncertainty in the law operates to the benefit of the defendant. Unless and until the Supreme Court of the United States expressly rejects a broadened interpretation of § 1443, that section will remain a viable and valuable tool for the male divorce defendant.

I believe, and hope, that reevaluation is beginning. Perhaps the ruling in the *Patterson* case, although it didn't give him everything he sought, was a starting place.

An order of remand entered in a case removed under 28 U.S. Code § 1443 is appealable to the United States Court of Appeals.[32] If a stay is granted pending appeal, the state court is powerless to enter any orders against the defendant pending final determination of the appeal.

What if everything else fails?[33] Okay, I keep throwing facts of life in your face. Have some more . . . See, I never promised you a paved road to the secret high-country fishing hole.

If it all goes kaput—well, for a few hundred dollars you've bought probably a minimum of eight months

Here is a table of what the methods do and do not provide.

PROVIDES	Civil Rights Removal: 28 U.S. Code §1443	Federal Question Removal: 28 U.S. Code §1441	Three-Judge Court	State Court
Automatically stays state court proceedings	Yes	Yes	No	No
Must be begun within 30 days	Yes	Yes	No	No, but issue should be raised
Appeal if court denies relief	Yes, to U.S. Court of Appeals	No right of appeal. District court's decision is final.	Yes, to U.S. Supreme Court.	Yes, within state court system. But, right to go into federal court is waived.
Scope of issues	Denial of equal civil rights in state court is only issue. But, in answer, all issues may be raised as in state court. Thus, these other federal issues may be raised in answer.	All federal questions necessarily arising from the suit.	Suit to restrain state officials (trial judge, governor, attorney general) from enforcement of unconstitutional state law. Civil Rights Act of 1871.	Does not apply here.
Bond required	Yes	Yes	No	No
Federal ruling may be stayed pending state court decision	No	No	Yes	Does not apply

of *maybe* living in your house and of not paying alimony.

Remember, it's not like back taxes, and you can't be billed for the time the court worked on the case. So, say alimony would be two hundred a month and the house payment is the same (forgetting for now the car and utilities), you've saved about twenty-five hundred dollars!

So, even if you lose—you win.

But, with the changing mood of the country and our laws (the Equal Rights Amendment), there's a better and better chance you'll win.

Chapter XVI

SOME FACTS AND FIGURES

Divorce is big business. During 1974, around 970,000 American couples (nearly two million persons) called it quits.[1]

Under no-fault in 1973, Florida saw 80,357 "domestic relations" cases filed. It was reported that domestic relations cases in 1973 made up 51.15 percent of all civil cases reported filed in that state's circuit courts.[2]

In New York, another no-fault state, there were 57,815 divorce actions filed between July 1973 and June 1974.[3]

For a change of pace, Illinois is one of the most populous states that is *not* a no-fault jurisdiction. That state had 44,671 divorces in 1973.[4]

A few representative statistics are provided in this chapter, to give you an idea of what is happening in the North, East, South, and West. Some states' statistics are more complete than others'. Most states simply do not keep in-depth records on who got what and so forth in divorce cases.

Nevertheless, I think you will find what is available most interesting. Patterns do appear.

We'll begin by using the latest figures from divorce actions in the State of Colorado. We see a definite trend (as economists say).

Not all the information on divorce actions was reported for 1972 (and even less was reported for 1973), but what was reported by the state court administrator's office might surprise even women's liberationists.

In 6,488 of the cases reported, the wife was the one who filed for divorce. Of those, 380 suits were dropped or otherwise dismissed, but a whopping 6,108 got their divorces.[5]

On the other hand, 2,162 men asked for divorces and 113 were turned down or otherwise had their cases dismissed—almost the same 6 percent when compared to the number of female complainants whose cases were dismissed.

Only eight cases were reported in which both the husband and wife wanted out. Interestingly, six of those requests were dropped or denied by the courts. That means only two of those eight couples who jointly asked for divorces got them.

Could it be that in the eyes of the courts, a couple who can agree that they can't get along can find some way to live together?

Those figures don't show discrimination. However, maybe they show that men are willing to put up with more from their wives than the wives are from the husbands. Or, trying to be fair, maybe there's the slightest chance that all those women filing for divorce had good reasons.

Back to business. Now for a blatant example of discrimination against men by divorce courts in a state that is considered to be a leader in the introduction of liberal legal ideas:

In the same available 1972 divorce information from Colorado, there were 5,058 cases in which children were involved.

In those 5,058 cases the wife got custody in 4,358 of them. The children were split between the husband and wife in 449 cases.

Why bother with percentages in the "wife-got" cases? What is of importance here is that in all those 5,058 cases, men got custody in only 251 cases—just under 5 percent![6]

It cannot be stressed too much that Colorado is a progressive state in divorce law. Therefore, if you don't live in that or a similar forward-moving state, imagine what the figures must look like where you abide!

The sexist discrimination visited upon males by the divorce courts of this nation is dehumanizing.

Like his black predecessor, the male who feels he is discriminated against in the state divorce courts has three options: (1) he may allow the state courts, applying state law, to emasculate him without so much as a whimper; (2) he may seek relief in the state appellate system, at great cost and possibly without success[7]; or (3) he may pay his fifteen dollars and nominal (in relation to alimony and the other horrors) attorney fees and seek relief in federal court.

I hope by now that you are fully aware that it is with the last choice that this book is concerned.

Something to keep in mind during your court fight is that you are treading on new ground—in the eyes of some judges. Your lawyer's job will be to convince the judges that court cases dealing with the general concepts or ideas you are trying to get across *do* apply in your case—even though the past cases did not deal specifically with divorce.

Again, the following additional divorce statistics may be used by your attorney to develop a pattern of nationwide discrimination against men, despite laws prohibiting such prejudice.

For local statistics in your area, you may have to build your own figures directly from the individual divorce-case files available for public inspection at your county courthouse. Or you can try using pretrial discovery to force the other side to do the work. A federal court could find it inexcusable that your state's judicial administrator keeps no embarrassing figures on alimony or child custody.

Missouri and then California have the most differentiated, detailed and extensive divorce information in the United States. Due to locally different methods of record keeping, statistics for Illinois, Florida, and New York, for example, are much more limited than those for Colorado, California, and Missouri.

Before no-fault in California, there were 69,299 divorces in 1969.[8] By 1973, under no-fault, that figure had climbed to 112,900.[9]

In California, the statistics show to whom the decree was granted. In 1969, the latest year for which such information is available, divorce decrees were awarded to 14,014 husbands, 54,767 wives, jointly to both parties in 492 instances, and in 26 cases it was not recorded who was granted the decree.[10]

Even more detailed statistics from 1966 show that in California (and probably nationally) the possibility of divorce is highest in the first four years of marriage (excluding the period before the first anniversary). Up to the first year, the odds are rather low, and after the fourth year they begin to decrease steadily.[11]

Another fact:

The divorce rates are higher, up through the ninth year of marriage, where the wife works outside the home.

The figures indicate that if your marriage can survive with your wife working outside the home through the first nine years, you may relax a little. From that point on, the rate of divorce for women working outside the home is lower than the rate for women who do not work outside the home.

In the 1966 statistics, a total of 23,295 housewives were involved in divorce cases, and 76,241 women working outside the home received divorces.

The one-to-four-year group included 6,513 housewives and 25,587 women with other occupations.

In the five-to-nine group, the housewife figures

dropped to 5,265, and the other-occupation stats were 15,591.

The average length of marriages was 7.0 years for housewives, and 5.0 for outside-working wives.[12]

Marriages with no children lasted 2.1 years in both categories, and in those with children younger than 18 years, the length was 8.0 for housewives and 7.6 for otherwise occupied women. Where children older than 18 years were involved, housewives' marriages lasted 25.4 years, and other-occupation wives' marriages lasted 24.5 years.[13]

In California, Illinois, Missouri, and quite a few other states, remarriage terminates the wife's right to receive alimony. The law is not clear everywhere. Sometimes the alimony terminates automatically upon remarriage. In other states, the first husband must file a motion with the court to terminate alimony, which motion the court *must* grant. In yet other states, the court *should* grant the motion unless there are "exceptional circumstances" (she married a poor man). In yet other states, such as New Jersey, Massachusetts, Oregon, and Nebraska, remarriage is grounds for no more than a possible reduction of the amount of alimony on the basis of a change in the ex-wife's financial circumstances.[14] Remarriage of the husband, however, nowhere terminates *his* obligation to pay alimony.

Some states expressly forbid the award of alimony to a man.[15] But even where the man theoretically is eligible, in actual practice only the women get the alimony. And statistics from Colorado and Missouri show that the women usually get the children.

Missouri is now a no-fault state. In 1973, 21,670 divorces were granted in Missouri. Of these, the husband was the plaintiff in 5,509 instances, and the wife in 16,115 instances. When the husband filed for divorce, he won 81.7 percent of the time. When the wife filed for divorce, she won 98.7 percent of the time.[16]

Missouri is probably the only state still keeping tabs

on custody awards. As one might expect, out of 12,114 cases involving children, men received custody in only 776 cases, compared to 10,829 cases in which women received custody.[17] There were 281 cases in which joint custody was awarded, 44 cases in which other custody arrangements were made, and in 184 cases the court decision concerning children was not stated. In gross figures, the husband won custody 6.4 percent of the time. When the husband was the one filing for divorce, his chances were better: he won custody of the children 21.7 percent of the time. But when the wife was the one filing for divorce, she won custody of the children 94.7 percent of the time.[18]

Of 107 annulments in Missouri in 1973, the wife received custody in just one case. In the other 106 cases, there were no children.[19]

That year in Missouri, wives got alimony in 11,560 cases, compared to—of course—zero for husbands.[20] The interesting thing in Missouri is that the alimony rate wasn't simply somewhat lower for men than for women—it was zero for men.

In two annulment cases, the court directed that alimony be paid to the person found *not* to be the wife.[21] (If an annulment determines that no marriage ever existed, one may wonder how the man logically can be expected to support his ex-nothing.)

The 1973 Missouri figures show 5,048 cases in which support to children was ordered, all in divorces. Alimony and child support was ordered in an additional 5,100 cases. Not one cent of alimony and child support was ordered paid to husbands.[22]

Missouri keeps the most complete divorce statistics of any state in the nation. The book entitled *Missouri Vital Statistics 1973,* published by the Missouri Center for Health Statistics, Post Office Box 570, Jefferson City, Missouri 65101, is a veritable indictment of the way the divorce courts are run in that state.

It's too bad the other states do not all maintain complete facts and figures.

As I've said before, federal courts have held that a showing of a statistical imbalance is good enough evidence to win a case of sexual discrimination.[23]

Chapter XVII

CHILD SUPPORT—YES, BUT . . .

Just because I disapprove of alimony, don't get the idea that I'm a complete monster. For instance, I think kids are neat.

A legitimate child (and most in divorce cases are legitimate) gives a man the prideful feeling of knowing part of him lives on. For this reason and out of love, men seem to have a prehistoric desire to see their children reach maturity.

I assume you are one of those men. You love your kids. You want to do right by them.

But you can't for the life of you understand why it should cost so much for your wife to raise the kids now that you're divorced. In a lot of cases, it shouldn't and it doesn't cost as much as you are paying to support the little rascals.

The support payments are unreasonably high. They're a cover for more "punishment" administered to you because you are a male.

There are methods of minimizing child support. Some of these apply if you are the biological or adoptive father of the child or children. Others apply if you are not the parent of the child in any way.

As I said earlier, most children are legitimate (or adopted). Therefore, I'm first going to talk about how to minimize child support in the case of legitimate kids.

Again, let's look at the equal rights part of the

whole thing. The proposed Equal Rights Amendment and the present federal civil rights laws are designed to force the traditionally male world of work to allow women to work.[1]

That's fine with you. Because if a woman has equal rights with a man (which is only right), she also, logically, has equal responsibilities (which also is only right).

What those two equalities mean to you is simply that your wife has the same responsibility as you do.[2] According to the Pennsylvania Supreme Court, that includes an equal share of the responsibility for the financial support of your kids. Equal employment opportunity carries with it equal support responsibility.[3]

Right there, your amount of the child-support payments should be cut in half. To back up the equal rights angle, we can again go to the Thirteenth Amendment which outlaws slavery, and to the federal civil rights law which prohibits peonage.[4]

Making you work to pay both your half of the child support *and* your wife's half is peonage.[5] An infringement upon your civil rights.

Before you go rushing off to court, read on. There's more you can do to minimize child support.

We're back to the old statistics. Even your eager lawyer might not be too thrilled with the actual gathering of these numbers, since these particular statistics have to be gathered from places other than the courts —figures on what it costs to raise a child.

I won't lie to you. All this research you're going to do may not do you any good. But it shouldn't hurt either, because at the very least you'll be finding out that your kids are getting enough to eat, and are getting shoes and clothing. And, at the very least, it will show that your ex-wife isn't living high off the hog by embezzling child-support money for perfume or some such.

Of course, there is still the other side of the coin.

The research could show that the kids are well taken care of, but that your ex-wife also is spending more than she earns at her job and/or (heaven forbid!) gets from you in the form of alimony. If she's spending more than comes in except for child support, where is the money coming from?

The "high living" money is coming out of the child-support payments, of course. And that is clear evidence that the payments are too much; obviously, because the kids are doing fine, and your ex-wife has to spend the extra money on *herself* just to use it up! If your state requires proof of a "change of circumstances" in order to lower support payments, the change of circumstances is that the extra money is no longer needed.

What the research you and your attorney are going to do will show (if it is the case) is that not only are your kids not doing without the necessities of life, but also from appearances your former spouse is living quite well—especially compared to you, and some of her neighbors.

The research should be done through a "disinterested party." A disinterested party is someone like a private detective—one who has a *good* reputation. (A good reputation in this kind of thing means the gumshoe is noted for honesty, and even in some cases for turning down clients who want him to do something shady.)

What are you going to research? How are you going to rake up the facts?

1. You check with the Census Bureau, and ask for any information pertaining to the cost of rearing children today. The U.S. Census Bureau maintains all kinds of statistics (or can refer you to other federal agencies). Their compilations are official government documents, and many courts will take "judicial notice" of them (that is, they can be admitted into evidence without

your having to bring in an expensive expert witness to testify).

2. You check with your local regional-planning or city-planning department to see if they have a recent survey or poll showing child-rearing costs. If they do, get certified copies and arrange to send a subpoena to the person who supervised the poll.

3. Contact local welfare and social-service agencies (both public and private) and find out what they believe is the cost of properly keeping a kid in necessities. (Don't overlook the point that most agencies feel it costs less for each extra child in one household.) If you find an agreeable social worker who feels a child can be raised for less than a fortune, arrange to have him or her subpoenaed as an expert witness.

4. Do your own door-to-door poll of residents in the area where your ex-wife lives, to see how much they spend on a kid. There are many companies across the country that specialize in doing surveys, and most of them can make up a survey which will accurately tell you what you want to know. But, again, check out such a company with your chamber of commerce or better business bureau before you hire them.

5. Get lists of nutritional requirements for a child the age of yours (from the U.S. Department of Agriculture or your state home extension office) and a list of food prices to fit those nutritional needs; get lists of clothing items, their costs, and life-expectancies; and hire an accountant to figure how much all that should cost along with projected medical and dental care (those figures often can be obtained from local medical and dental societies, which are listed in the Yellow Pages of your phone book or can be found simply by calling the office of a doctor or a dentist).

6. The detective—well, let's be honest—snoops around and generally spies on the ex-wife to find out what her life style is. You want an itemized, dated list, as closely as can be obtained, of what she buys, where

she buys it, when she buys it, and how much it costs. If you've got a good detective, don't be too disgusted if he informs you that he got merchandise prices by pawing through your ex's garbage cans. (He might charge extra for *that* service, and I don't know about you, but to me it's worth it.) The gumshoe also may discover, from the garbage can, that while you have hamburgers and TV dinners, your ex-wife is eating steak.

7. You organize all the information, and you have the accountant work up a comparison chart and a comparison list on each—on the child costs and support and on the former wife's earnings-alimony income and outgo.

8. The accountant's figures will show whether or not the ex-wife is spending more than the income intended for *her*, and it will show whether the child support you are paying is more than is necessary. Assuming the amounts are more in both cases, your attorney then will prepare a motion to the court for relief.

9. Your attorney then can send your ex-wife detailed written "interrogatories" (questions she must answer in writing under oath). And he can also arrange to take her "deposition" (cross-examine her under oath and inspect her financial records in advance of the court hearing, for the purpose of discovering what her testimony will be). The object is to get her to lie under oath about things you know you can refute at the court hearing. Things like the specifics of her claimed high cost of living.

In the motion to reduce child-support payments, your lawyer will of course refer to civil rights legislation, and tell the court that your civil rights are being violated, and how they are being violated.[6]

His motion might read something like this:

"Defendant, therefore, prays for relief from a portion of current court-ordered child-support payments. A reduction in support is sought on the grounds of a change in circumstances, to wit that defendant's present payments are grossly unreasonable in the light of current accepted living standards and appended research. Said relief further is sought on the grounds that current support appears to have been procured by plaintiff fraudulently by misrepresentations to this honorable court, for the purpose of enhancing her unearned income from defendant. Plaintiff has converted the child-support money obtained from defendant to her own personal use in direct violation of her duty to use said monies for the support of defendant's children, and in direct and callous disregard of the welfare of defendant's children."

Don't let yourself or your lawyer be misled by the apparent simplicity of the method. It isn't simple at all. It will take a lot of time to get the needed information about your kids, your ex-wife, your ex's neighbors, and about kids in general. And you and your attorney will spend a lot of sweat putting the information into a neat, accurate, easily understandable package for the court.

Don't foul it all up by being sloppy.

Now what about the case in which the ex-husband is paying support for a child carried by his wife while they were still married . . . but fathered by another man?

Under the law, you are *presumed* to be the father of any child your wife conceives during the existence of the marriage. But this presumption can be overcome.

Should you, that ex-husband, support the child? Would it be embarrassing to drag out the dirty linen, and admit to having been made to wear the horns?

First question first. If the child thinks you are its father, then it could be most harmful for the child to discover that it really is a bastard. Indeed, if the child is old enough to think you are its father, you probably have slept on your rights too long to successfully challenge paternity.

Out of concern for the welfare of the child, your lawyer should approach your ex-wife's and explain that you know the child is not yours. And, because of that, you don't think you should have to pay support for the child.

She and her attorney should be told quite plainly and without malice that if they do not agree to ending the support, you will feel forced to take the matter into open court. Which, you admit, would not be good for the child or for the child's image of its mother, and which you would not like at all—but which you will do if forced.

In a case where the child thinks you are the true father, a court might feel that it would be in the child's best interest to maintain the fiction. In such a case, the court might hold that you waited too long to question legitimacy. However, the court also might be inclined to lean your way in a request to make child support low, in view of your humanitarian compassion for the child.

That is, if you approach the court with the problem, saying that you know the child isn't yours, but you don't want to hurt the little tyke's self-image any more than the divorce already has. "However, dear judge, I just can't afford the outrageous support I'm forced to pay for another man's child."

In the case, your attorney will present to the court the same kind of information that is described earlier in the discussion for fathers of legitimate children.

The approach is genuine. You are admitting to the court that you want the support reduced. But you also care about the child. You especially don't think it's fair for your ex-wife to use the child dishonestly to obtain even more money by claiming the poor kid eats enough for five.

What if you haven't slept on your rights? (Time limits for questioning paternity vary from state to state.) What if the child was conceived around the time of the split-up?

In a few states, all it takes for the court to rule

that a child is illegitimate is the "father's" testimony that the kid isn't his.[7] Of course, the testimony must be believable to the court. In those states, courts accept as proof of bastardization the husband's sworn statement of nonaccess at the time of conception. Usually in cases such as that, you and your wife weren't sleeping together and hadn't been for quite a while, so you're sure it was not you who got her pregnant.[8] In some other states, proof of nonaccess must be by the testimony of a "disinterested witness."

In some states, it is considered proof that the child is a bastard if the child's blood type and your blood type do not match up biologically. And in other states this is not accepted,[9] but the constitutionality of a court's refusal to consider such evidence might present grounds for suit in federal court.[10]

At any rate, this approach requires blood tests and expert pathological testimony. And, because of the way human blood groups work out, the tests might end up showing that the child might or might not be yours. (A good high-school or college biology textbook will explain blood groups quite well.)

Another way of proving to the court that the child isn't yours is to find other men who had sexual relations with your wife at the time or about the time the child was conceived. If you were having relations with your wife at the time of conception, and the blood type tests show a maybe-yes, maybe-no on a match-up, then you have a poor legal case for bastardization. The burden is on you to rebut the presumption that the child is yours.

However, in such a situation, probably your best lever is to ask for custody of the child because the mother is unfit, and settle for a reduction in the amount of support you have to pay.

Of course, the foolproof way of proving nonaccess and ending support payments is to come up with the real father, and have him admit it under oath.

To summarize, though, courts in many states generally tend to lean toward the man's side in cases involving claims of illegitimacy (one of the few places where a man gets something resembling fairness in a divorce-related case). Where the man can't get a fair shake under state law, the federal courts may be receptive. However, rules of evidence and time limits for challenging legitimacy are stringent, and vary widely from state to state.

Chapter XVIII

ENDING ALIMONY?

Equal employment opportunity means equal support responsibility. In a job-discrimination case, a federal appeals court at New Orleans said that

> Title VII rejects just this kind of romantic paternalism as unduly Victorian and instead vests individual women with the power to decide whether or not to take on unromantic tasks. Men have always had the right to determine whether the incremental increase in remuneration for strenuous, dangerous, obnoxious, boring or unromantic tasks is worth the candle. The promise of Title VII is that women are now to be on equal footing.[1]

On the employment scene, it has been held that one sex may not be required to work longer hours than the other.[2] This principle ought to be equally applicable on the divorce scene. In *Burns* v. *Rohr Corporation*,[3] a federal court in California has ruled that a state regulation requiring rest breaks for women, but not for men, was discriminatory. In *Wilson* v. *Sibley Memorial Hospital*,[4] a federal court at Washington, D.C., held that a male nurse may not be denied the right to render services to female patients. And in *LeBlanc* v. *Southern Bell Telephone and Telegraph Company*,[5] another federal court ruled that the "treadworn assertion that there are differences between sexes, sociological, physiological and biological, justifying rational generic classification and that a prohibition on women working in excess of 8 hours a day or 48 hours a week as provided by Louisiana statute . . . constituted a stereotyped classification. . . ."[6]

President Ford has proclaimed that "Women's liberation is truly the liberation of all people." Equal rights carry equal responsibilities.[7]

Or, to say it another way: equal rights, equal support. The laws say we're equal, men and women. That means the woman is just as capable of supporting herself as is the man *and* she also is just as capable of supporting the children, if she gets custody in an equal-justice court.[8]

In 1974, Congress passed a law to protect consumers against unfair billing practices.[9] For our purposes, the second major provision of that law is the more important. That section prohibits lenders from discriminating against women in credit transactions on the basis of sex *or* marital status.[10]

This is one more indication that under the law, women have the same rights as men—for instance, the right to support themselves *and* to be able to borrow money to purchase luxuries or merely to try to make ends meet. Many men who are paying alimony find themselves in the position of having to borrow money (either occasionally or often) to make payments. Those loans would not be necessary if the men were not paying alimony. So, why not simply eliminate the middleman and let the woman do the borrowing—to pay her rent?

The least you should settle for is an equal division of the cost of supporting children and no alimony!

Maybe men should file a class-action suit demanding reparations for the divorce atrocities of the past . . .[11]

And when it comes to a "division of property" such as the house, why does it always have to go to the wife? I cannot find a logical reason for the house title to go to the wife, when the husband (in most cases) paid for the house.[12] If courts insist on giving custody of children to women, the least they can do is honor the way we look at purchases in our society—outside divorce court. You know, when you plunk your money down on the counter, what you bought belongs to you.

All right. There are children involved in the marriage, and consequently, in the divorce. The court for some reason decides to give permanent custody of the children to the wife.

Why does she have to have title to the house? Why can't the court find it in its infinite wisdom to order, at the worst, that the house be used on a lease basis, with the house going back to the husband after the children reach an age at which they reasonably can be expected to leave home, or when the woman remarries?

The court can do that. And, if the kids aren't ready to move out into the cold, cruel world at age eighteen or whatever, well, you can either simply allow them to stay in the house or you can charge them rent.

This approach is more than reasonable. Look at it this way:

Mr. Doe has a job. He doesn't owe anybody any money. He has a very nice reclining armchair, which he purchased with cash, and for which he has a receipt.

Mr. Apple, who is a neighbor of Mr. Doe, has liked old Doe for years. But he suddenly decides that he no longer likes Doe, and also that he wants that reclining armchair Doe has in his den.

So, Mr. Apple goes to court. He tells the judge, "Your honor, I do not like my neighbor, Mr. Doe, to whom I have lived next door for more than thirty years. Therefore, and based upon my admitting that I don't like Doe, I demand that you make him give me that sharp reclining armchair that he bought."

In your regular court, Mr. Apple might be bound over for psychiatric study. Everybody knows you can't just take away somebody else's property just because you don't like him. Right?

But what if regular court was run like a divorce court? Why, then Mr. Apple's logic would be the logic of the court. In divorces, the way to decide if the wife gets the house is to determine that she can't stand the sight of her husband anymore. Apple said in court that he now dislikes Doe, didn't he? Okay. Running the regular court like a divorce court, the judge would tell Doe to give that armchair to Mr. Apple, because Mr. Apple doesn't like Mr. Doe anymore.

Make sense? Of course not. Let's change the approach, then, in divorce so it makes sense.

Chapter XIX

YES, THEY'RE MARRIED

Let's talk about the man who already is paying alimony to an ex-wife who is living with another man. And the other man is helping her spend the alimony.

Under the eyes of the law they live in a state of "de facto remarriage." This is similar to the idea of common-law marriage, but is applicable even in states that don't recognize common-law marriages.

Many states have some form of common law which says that persons who live together as man and wife for a period of time are married.

There is some debate about how the system of common-law marriage came to be accepted in this country. But it's easy to understand. Consider the people on the early frontiers. Back in those days, men and women met and fell in love and wanted to get married. But the preacher rode a circuit, and might not get back to the lovers' area for maybe a year.

What to do? Well, there were two choices. The happy couple could try to look but not touch until the preacher got around. That occasionally led to babies out of wedlock. So, often in an isolated area the enamored declared themselves bound to each other, and lived together until the parson got around again and married them legally.

This type of situation was common. It was accepted by members of remote communities as all right—not quite as good as chasing the Bible-man and doing it right the first time, but better than sneaking around. It showed that the couple accepted the rules of the country, and it showed that they had good intentions.

(If records where you live, in areas that once were frontiers, were checked, it might be discovered that some of the oldest pioneer families arose from couples who never were "legally" married by a preacher. They might have been waiting for him, but the parson might have been set upon by Indians or more likely by bandits. And, by the time the preacher or a replacement got around, there were children. So, to avoid marking the kids as bastards or at the least a lot early, there just wasn't any ceremony and everyone in the community understood and nobody was critical. Not if he or she had good sense. For who knew but that somewhere in his or her own past there was a similar "marriage.")

Another thing—the announcement, or the open living together, indicated to friends and relatives that the couple planned to care for each other and to provide for the proper rearing of any children. Relatives (admittedly, mostly those of the woman) were especially concerned that the new couple be thought of as "married up."

Thus, common-law marriage came to be an accepted part of Americana. But as time passed and civilization came to the frontier, some states (but not all) passed laws prohibiting common-law marriages. And at least one state, Louisiana, with its French law tradition, has never considered common-law marriages binding.

However, two cases of Louisiana origin have outmoded the previous Louisiana way of looking at common-law marriages in some instances. Interestingly enough, the cases—not related other than in subject matter—both were decided by the United States Supreme Court on May 20, 1968.

In those cases, *Levy* v. *Louisiana*[1] and *Glona* v.

American Guarantee and Liability Insurance Company,[2] the Supreme Court looked to the actual relationships of the persons involved in the suits, although both cases centered around illegitimate children. Lower courts had ruled that as "illegitimate children" they had no legally recognizable connection-rights to the mothers involved.

In each case, the Supreme Court held that mere social, outmoded considerations about illegitimacy could not override the verifiable fact of a relationship and bond between the mothers and their children.

In *Levy* v. *Louisiana*,[3] the Court ruled that the circumstances under which five illegitimate children lived with their mother, and not the fact that they were born out of wedlock, governed whether the children had been deprived of the mother's care and support.

The children were suing for damages in the wrongful death of their mother, Louise Levy. The high Court overruled lower courts which had said the children had no right to damages as a result of their mother's death because the children had been born out of wedlock. The lower courts' decisions were based upon Louisiana law governing the rights of parents and children where illegitimacy is involved.

In the *Glona* case,[4] Minnie Glona was suing for damages in the wrongful death of her illegitimate son.

The suit first was brought in the United States District Court for the Eastern District of Louisiana. It was dismissed on the ground that Louisiana law gives no right of action to the mother for the death of an illegitimate child. The United States Court of Appeals for the Fifth Circuit upheld the decision, but—again—the United States Supreme Court reversed the lower court and said that courts should look to the *fact* of familial relationships for finding the rights in the cases, and not to the legal status of the relationships, such as illegitimacy or the lack of a "legal" marriage.

When the Supreme Court overturned the cases, it

was suggesting that men and women, even though not legally married, had a "de facto" marital relationship that the state was required to recognize. And the concept of a federal common-law marriage was born under a new name—de facto marriage.

If your ex-wife is living with another man and is sharing expenses or household duties with him, then they are not just living together—according to court rulings, they have entered into a de facto marriage.

What if they are maintaining separate apartments, but in fact are spending the time together at one of the apartments?

I think a private detective could show that they have entered into a quasi-marital relationship, although they have not in fact gotten married and have not entered into a common-law marriage.

You've got the general drift by now, but you want to know more? Let's start with "de facto."

De facto translates loosely to "by fact," or even more loosely to "by actions or circumstances." Therefore, what a "de facto remarriage" means is that although your ex-wife and her friend haven't been pronounced man and wife by a clergyman or judge, they are *acting* as if they are married. And, as the U.S. Supreme Court has said, the states must recognize the actual family relationships, even if your state doesn't permit common-law marriages.

In 1959, the Ohio Supreme Court held in the case of *Hunt* v. *Hunt*[5] that remarriage of the ex-wife terminates alimony requirements. The court cited a New Mexico case to make its point. Quoting the New Mexico Supreme Court's decision in *Kuert* v. *Kuert,*[6] the Ohio court said:

A contrary decision would result in what might well be described as: quasi-polygamy by court order.[7]

Ohio's highest state court then went on to say:

[I]t is the conclusion of this court, that it is contrary to good public policy to require a divorced wife's former husband to continue to make alimony payments to her after her subsequent marriage to another man capable of supporting her, and that such marriage constitutes an election on her part to be supported by her new husband and an abandonment of the provision for permanent alimony from her divorced husband, and reservation of jurisdiction is implied so that the equitable power of the court may be invoked to modify its order accordingly.[8]

The 1973 case of *Fahrer* v. *Fahrer*[9] entered Ohio's Circuit Court at Cincinnati on a show-cause order demanding that the defendant give a good reason why he should not be held in contempt of court for failure to pay installments of alimony ($400 a month, by stipulation or agreement).

Testimony showed that after the couple was divorced in 1966, the plaintiff (ex-wife) moved to Florida and commenced cohabiting with another man. It was also shown that common-law marriages are not recognized in Florida, although they are in Ohio.

The court found the defendant's former wife had entered into a relationship which, if maintained in Ohio, would constitute a common-law marriage.

Therefore, the court ruled in favor of the *ex*-husband and treated the woman as having remarried. The Ohio Court of Appeals affirmed. Said the court:

We hold that the plaintiff has entered into a relationship with a man which if maintained in Ohio would constitute a valid marriage and, therefore, she must be said to have remarried within the meaning of the agreement made part of the decree.[10]

There are at least fourteen states that recognize common-law marriages, and which should therefore be highly amenable to the excellent logic of the *Fahrer* decision. These states are: Alabama, Colorado, Georgia,

Idaho, Iowa, Kansas, Montana, Ohio, Oklahoma, Pennsylvania, Rhode Island, South Carolina, Texas, and the District of Columbia.[11]

Please note that although some states (such as Louisiana) do not recognize common-law marriages, they (like Louisiana in *Levy* and *Glona*) may be forced to recognize de facto relationships.

In some states, alimony terminates automatically upon the remarriage of the woman. Of course, again, variations exist. The alimony termination is not automatic in some places, and the man must file a motion with the court. Elsewhere, a divorced woman's remarriage is grounds for a reduction of alimony only. And some states do not clearly fit into any one category.[12]

Two states, however, rigidly enforce the "must terminate" rule: California and Illinois.[13] And some states appear to fluctuate in practice, from court to court and even from case to case in the *same* court. North Dakota and Utah are quite aboveboard about being "must terminate" states—but with the caveat that some or all alimony may be continued under "exceptional circumstances."[14] Unfortunately, a man going into court to try and get alimony off his back, has no way in the world of knowing what a particular judge will consider to be an "exceptional circumstance." The judge's view may depend upon what he had for breakfast.

If you know your former wife is living with the man, and has been for quite a while, and you have witnesses, you can use this information to have a good go at getting your ex-wife's alimony cut off. You do this by having your attorney petition the court to order the alimony requirement terminated because your former wife has entered into another "marriage."

Your lawyer should refer to as many previous de-facto-remarriage rulings as he can come up with.[15] And your lawyer should emphasize that although your ex-wife's new "marriage" is not orthodox, it is accepted as a marriage by the courts and it also is becoming a modern substitute for old-fashioned marriage.

Also, for a court to order you to support your ex-wife is unconstitutional, but for a court to order you to support your former wife *and* her new husband is . . . well, it's just downright unbelievable! As the New Mexico Supreme Court said, it would be "quasi-polygamy by court order."[16]

"Of course your Honor is quite unaware of the re-marriage of my client's ex-wife, or we know the alimony would have been ended long ago," your attorney will tell the judge.

"We know your Honor is perfectly aware of the Thirteenth Amendment to the Constitution of the United States, which says, 'Neither slavery nor involuntary servitude . . . shall exist within the United States. . . .' "

Your lawyer then will explain that it is a pure case of slavery to force you to pay alimony to your ex-wife so she and her new "husband" can live in luxury. And your attorney will—of course—ask the judge to rescind the order telling you to pay alimony.

Your lawyer will point out how much you would hate to have to go into U.S. District Court with a civil rights complaint. He should point out the grounds for such a complaint (as outlined in Chapter XIV), and might tell the local judge that you realize the local judge is aware of the fact that everyone has civil rights.

And, of course, the local judge is as concerned as anyone with protecting civil rights. So, you expect a quick ruling in your favor.

Your lawyer should do his best to make the tone of his memorandum and request for relief one of simple explanation of things well known to all. You don't want it to sound like blackmail, because it really isn't.

You see, blackmail is holding something over someone's head in order to gain something else that doesn't rightfully belong to you. What you're trying to get rightfully belongs to you.

Speaking of things that rightfully belong to you, your lawyer also should demand that your ex-wife and her friend pay back any and all alimony you paid to her after the new marriage. For her to keep the money would be fraud. She got it by deceit—by not telling the court she had remarried.

And, if you're feeling particularly nasty, you can file a separate action against your ex-wife and her de facto husband for obtaining money by fraud!

Now, if your lawyer (who should be able to find out) thinks you can't get a fair shake in local court, go straight to federal court.

In federal court, you file a civil rights complaint on the same basis mentioned earlier—the Thirteenth Amendment guarantee of freedom from slavery. You follow almost the same procedure as that outlined in Chapter XIV, only you aim it at the fact that you are being deprived of your rights by slavery and peonage. And you point out that no woman is forced into this kind of servitude, so you again are being discriminated against because you are a man. And you charge that your state's courts refuse to recognize de facto remarriages in violation of the Fourteenth Amendment as applied in the *Levy* and *Glona* cases.[17] And you sue your ex-wife and her new love for obtaining money "under color of state law" in violation of your federal rights to have their de facto remarriage recognized in the state courts, to be free from involuntary servitude and peonage, and to be treated without sexual discrimination.

It won't hurt to let the federal court know you're serious about this thing by having a fraud action pending on the local level against your ex-wife and her new husband, too.

Oh, yes, don't let your lawyer try to hide out behind

calling your wife's new husband "alleged husband," or some other beat-around-the-bush term. As I've explained, they're married. For better or worse. Worse for them, and much, much better for you!

Chapter XX

FOR THE NEXT TIME

An awful lot of divorced people get married again, only to get divorced again. Does that mean the whole rigmarole is like shooting craps?

As best as I can tell you about love, the answer appears to be yes.

But, as for having to go through the divorce hassle again, the answer is no.

My suggestion, even for those who have never been divorced, but who are getting married, is to write up a marriage contract—with a lawyer's help, of course.

Some years ago when a friend of mine got married, his wife was pretty independent. She said she would not go along with the part of the marriage ceremony (religious) which binds the wife to "obey" her husband. As an alternative, they agreed to omit the word "obey" from the ceremony, and agreed to discuss all major issues and to make joint decisions about them.

Further, they agreed verbally to certain conditions in the event of a divorce. Examples were equal division of property, such as paintings and furniture, with tough "who-gets-this" decisions made by a flip of a coin.

In the event there were children, they agreed the husband would pay support—reasonable support—and would have reasonable visiting rights, including such important days as birthdays and Christmas.

It was verbally agreed that at such time as a divorce occurred, they would decide whether to sell the house and fairly divide the proceeds, or whether the woman would keep the house to shelter children, or whether the man would keep the house because the woman did not need it or did not wish to have it or because the man needed it to shelter the children in the event the woman did not want custody.

It was agreed that in the event of no children, not only would the man expect the wife to pursue her career as a teacher to support herself, but also, she said she would prefer that to taking his charity!

Through his own choice, the man agreed that if there were young children, he would rather pay some alimony for a few years so the mother would not have to farm out the children. In that way, they reasoned, the mother could rear the children herself, instead of having someone else do the job, possibly not to the liking of either parent.

However, their verbal agreement was that when the children were going to school all day, it would be time for the woman to go back to work full time and take over her own support again.

I consider that a more than fair agreement, which shows the love of the two people for each other and which shows their concern for the welfare of their children.

Of course, to some it might look like the couple was planning to get divorced. However, to me it looks like they didn't think they would ever be divorced, but they wanted to be sure to have a rational plan for handling the situation. They realized that in the heat of a divorce some couples sink to the level of trying to see who can hurt whom the most.

If they do divorce—and I don't foresee that, because they talk things out as per agreement—it is likely they won't be among the embittered divorced persons. They will be able to go into another marriage with the view that not all marriages work out, but neither does a divorce have to lead to lifelong misery and poverty.

Although their agreement is verbal, and each intends to keep the agreement, I personally—being a cynic, and also a lawyer—prefer written contracts. That way, you don't forget what's in the agreement.

The two of you will have to decide what your contract will include. You may get ideas from the earlier chapters of this book, and also from my description of my friend's agreement with his wife.

Have your lawyer draw it up, as you would a will, and have it signed and witnessed or notarized legally.[1]

Keep in mind the civil rights laws, so you don't end up agreeing to something that cannot be upheld in court. And bear in mind that you cannot contract away your obligation to do your share of supporting your children. They are not parties to the contract, and cannot be bound by it. Your wife, however, is a party to the contract. In most states, such contracts are binding.

A recent item in the *American Bar Association Journal* stated:

> Changes in society's views toward the husband-wife relationship should prompt more interest in these agreements. A contract altering the husband's duty of support should have a more receptive audience today than just a few years ago.[2]

When each of you knows what he or she will get out of a divorce—part of everything, but not all of everything—you may find it much easier to remain married. And relatively happy.

With the forming of the contract, you and your wife (in many states you can do this if you're already married, too) begin to learn to work things out together, and to respect each other.

Chapter XXI

SO, DO SOMETHING!

In 1839, Theodore Dwight Weld and his wife, Angelina Grimké, published an abolitionist work, *Slavery as It Is,* which later provided inspiration for Harriet Beecher Stowe's *Uncle Tom's Cabin,* and for a portion of Charles Dickens's *American Notes.*[1] The spread of the active antislavery movement has been attributed to followers of Weld, called the greatest abolitionist.[2]

The Welds' paper was based on eyewitness accounts of the cruelties of slavery in pre–Civil War America. Interestingly enough, the statement of purpose of the work uses descriptive terminology that today may be applied to the plight of the slaves of divorce:

> We will prove that the slaves in the United States are treated with barbarous inhumanity; that they are overworked, underfed, wretchedly clad and lodged, and have insufficient sleep; that they are often made to wear round their necks iron collars armed with prongs, to drag heavy chains and weights at their feet while working in the field and to wear yokes, and bells, and iron horns . . . that they are often hunted with bloodhounds.[3]

Comparisons easily are made between the black slaves of the nineteenth century and the divorce slaves of the twentieth. It would, technically, be hyperbole to attempt to apply the quotation directly to the lot of divorced men. But, if we break down the work into segments, and apply them with explanation, the accuracy easily is seen.

I think the statistics and other information in this book have pretty well proven that male divorce refugees are "treated with barbarous inhumanity," and worse, with callous disregard for established rights that did not even exist at the time of black slavery.

Divorced men of today in many cases "are overworked, underfed, wretchedly clad and lodged." They pay so much in alimony, child support, house and car payments, and in life and health insurance premiums that they become, in effect, workhorses, producing far more in life than they are allowed to receive. All you have to do is look at the poor fellows to see that they are underfed and wretchedly clad. Just as they haven't the funds to dine and attire themselves as do their married and single friends, they also quite often live in apartments which roaches would be embarrassed to list as home.

The bit about iron collars and dragging heavy chains and weights is a magnificent, poetic, figurative representation of the divorced man's situation. He has been ordered by a court of law to keep his job and work for the benefit of his ex-wife . . . and if that isn't a heavy chain, an example of being made "to wear yokes," then none may be found.

It is conceivable that some sheriffs' officers and private detectives will take exception, but I feel no qualms about pointing out that what happened to runaway slaves in the nineteenth century is exactly what happens to a twentieth-century divorce slave if he fails to make a payment[4]—he is "often hunted with bloodhounds." The runaway slave when caught was either shot, or taken back and whipped or otherwise physically punished. Today's divorce slave is brought before the bench, given a tongue-lashing, and sometimes even sent to jail (which is interesting, since if the ex-wife needs the income so badly, how can she afford to have the money factory locked up where he won't have any way to make the money to give to her?).

It is unfortunate that the same news media that apprised us of Watergate allow themselves to be exploited for essentially the same purposes that once were served by the whippings that were administered to the slaves of old: public ridicule. Newspapers, which at the first hint of censorship point to the Constitution, totally ignore that venerable document in the case of men charged with "nonsupport."

Yes, nonsupport cases are good copy. The articles point out in lurid detail how Ralph B., who works at Imaginary Products, Inc., and earns $142 a week, failed to pay his ex-wife the court-ordered sum of $300 last month.

It is saddening to note that the newspapers, which in many other areas have been the support pillars of civil rights, fail to report some of the side issues in the nonsupport cases. For instance:

If we say the $142 is Ralph B.'s take-home pay, he earns $568 a month. When $300 is subtracted from that, the leftovers are $268.

If Ralph's rent is $100 a month (try to find an apartment with anything for that in even a moderately sized city), he then has $168. We (like Ralph) should not forget his utility bills, which may be $50, which leaves $118.

Ralph, as do the rest of us, has a habit acquired early in life. He is in the habit of eating. Bachelors and divorced men are notorious among mothers and sisters for not cooking meals for themselves. Ralph is no exception. Conservatively, his café bill averages out to $2 per meal.

If Ralph eats three meals a day, the cost is $6. There are seven days in the week, and that multiplied by the $6-a-day meal cost totals $42. Using a basic, four-week month, that means his meals cost him $168 a month.

Oh? He only had $118 left after his alimony, rent, and utility payments? Well, how about that.

Golly, gee, your Honor, Ralph spent $50 more than he was supposed to have left for food. No, not really.

What Ralph does most months is just cut out enough meals to keep such frivolous expenditures to a minimum. His approach, you see, is just to not eat breakfast for twenty-five days of each month. Actually, he skips breakfast more often than that because he likes to have pocket money in case he feels like going on a tear and buying a cup of coffee.

Besides, emergencies come up. Like broken shoelaces. Ralph likes to keep some cash on hand for things like that because his fellow workers are squeamish about lending amounts of capital large enough to cover replacement of the laces.

Ralph is a bad credit risk. He travels for the company sometimes, and therefore has to have a car. Last time the aged—but stately, he insists—auto broke down, Ralph went to his neighborhood Loan Center.

The nice man with the knife-scarred face told Ralph that Loan Center couldn't take a chance on him. The man suggested that Ralph learn to handle his money more wisely. Well, Ralph has that down to a science. He just skipped several dinners each week (skipping dinner saves more money because lunch is the cheaper meal).

I beg your pardon? "Ralph used up all his money on alimony, rent, utilities, and food, and how can he pay for gas for his car?"

That is exactly the question Ralph frequently asks himself.

Another item the papers fail to tell us is the extent of the paralysis of Ralph's ex-wife. Naturally, we assume she is paralyzed or in some other way incapacitated so she cannot support herself by working. Of course, we still wonder why she is not on welfare instead of Ralph-care . . .

You may stop holding your breath. Your concern for the poor woman is touching, but I must tell you that, actually, she is not in any way encumbered. Not in any way. But if that's what you say, then you are not a man faced with a divorce suit (or wondering what he would do if his wife wanted a divorce). If you can say that, at this point in this book, you are probably one of my fellow attorneys and you are not being honest with yourself; you are a clergyman of a faith that believes in punishing men for allowing a divorce to happen; or you are a woman who doesn't want to face the fact that she might have to get out and do a little of the old Bring-Home-the-Bacon-Shuffle.

By now, I hope you are feeling akin to that child on the summer day who wants to do *something*. There are steps one may take other than simply fighting one's own divorce case in the federal courts.

Even single men and still-married men may join in demanding a National Divorce Law based upon the Thirteenth and Fourteenth Amendments and upon the thinking of the Equal Rights Amendment. Please notice that I didn't say "ask" for a national divorce law. We will have to demand it, or we won't get it. We must make it clear to our congressmen that such a law will serve two equal-rights purposes: it will give men a fair shake in divorce actions, and it will ensure that divorced women will receive their guaranteed right to work.

If we had a national divorce law, a man would know just exactly what to expect in divorce court in every town in every state in the Union. Of course, if the national divorce law as proposed is not fair, the congressmen will receive even more telephone calls, telegrams, letters, and personal consultations from and by their constituents—until they get it right!

"Grass roots" is a term heard quite often lately.

It means beginning at the bottom of the political heap —you and me.

A grass-roots campaign may be begun to defeat the local divorce judges if they persist in making bigoted decisions that infringe upon the rights of men to be free from slavery. If a judge is particularly obnoxious in his divorce rulings, it may become necessary to recall him. Any fairly competent attorney can advise you of the procedure for recalling an elected official. In fact, if you have a county attorney on the government payroll, he has the duty to answer your questions about such things.

You may be sure that within fifteen minutes of your posing the question about recalling Judge So-And-So, the judge will know about it. His rulings may change dramatically after that—especially if he is given a hint about what you think he is doing wrong. Perhaps a fairly understandable and quite permissible "hint" would be to send the judge a copy of this book as an exhibit to your brief.

Aside from selling one more copy of the book for me, having it in front of him will enable him to make sure he looks up the right laws and cases. I do not think it immodest to say that if the judge will take the trouble to look up the citations in this book, he will begin to change his views about divorce immediately.

It is bad for a judge's image to be constantly removing himself from cases. And, when the eager young lawyers (even those eighty years young) get hold of a procedure, such as the one mentioned earlier that involves suing the local judge, it becomes politically expedient for the good judge to reevaluate decisional divorce law as handed down from his bench. Judges know that people quickly lose faith in a jurist who spends a good deal of his time in federal court, trying to explain why so many men think he is discriminatory in his divorce rulings. When people lose faith, judges lose votes.

Recently, persons have been reviving the old idea of a thing that has come to be called, among other names, "contract cohabitation." The method here is that a man (or woman) hires someone to live with him and cook and do household chores that a wife would normally take care of. Just what is expected of each is spelled out in a written contract.

Understandably, it has an appeal for the divorced man (who thinks he can afford it). Divorced men are a little leery of remarriage—although as the statistics show, they remarry more often than do women[5]—and are seeking alternative arrangements whereby they may receive companionship and other services thought of in connection with the title "wife," without actually having to get married or simply live with someone.

Proponents of contract cohabitation claim the arrangement is legitimized in the eyes of snoopy, elderly women in next-door apartments when it is explained that the couple is not "shacking up"; nothing as common as that, it is a business arrangement.

However, the word "common" brings to mind common-law marriage. Common-law marriage would not occur under the arrangement in most states simply because most states recognizing common-law marriages require that the couple represent themselves as man and wife—which they definitely are not doing under a C.C.

But, there are some states which will say, "We find all of this talk of contracts in terms of household duties rather suspicious." And then the court (at the urging of police vice-squad officers, the district attorney, and the woman next door who, after all, was not convinced) just might say the arrangement was one of lewd cohabitation, despite the written contract.

The C.C. probably would be upheld on any of a number of bases, among them invasion of privacy.

At any rate, if you are considering such a move, it would be wise to be aware that problems might result. It also would be wise to consult an attorney before you get involved in contract cohabitation.

Group or "corporate" marriage also has been a topic of conversation for about ten years. The premise here is that a family unit of two or more couples, with enabling state or even federal legislation, could incorporate.

The incorporated family then would provide a distribution of the work- and support-loads. The couples would share a large house, and would share incomes and household chores, as well as providing for two or more conversation-discussion-decision-making sex partners for each member of the corporation. It has been suggested that such an arrangement might in time cut the divorce rate.

One view is that such an incorporation provides more than the obvious sexual advantages. It is offered that the incorporation would give those involved a larger and therefore more stable family-group base. One suggested advantage in the incorporated family is that the children will adapt more quickly to the addition of two new "parents" than they would to the subtraction of one parent and the addition of one new parent. That is, it is argued, the children remain with both original parents, and acquire two new ones besides.

Thus, the children would have the opportunity to receive adult input and supervision from four individuals or more, and a chance for greater adult-role review. Persons discussing the concept seem to arrive at the idea (after they calm down) that with that many "parents" in the home, a child might have a better chance of finding a sympathetic ear.

Of course, there are those who faint at the proposal. Under such an arrangement, they argue, the children will become warped and will get a totally distorted view of the world. Which would be quite true if the corporation operated successfully. Children would see a number of adults cooperating in a venture on a warm and (according to the plan) loving level. Now, *that* definitely is a warped view.

I myself would prefer not to advocate communal living arrangements. But their current conceptual (and apparent actual) popularity as an alternative to traditional family life surely suggests that the courts have made the institution of marriage tragically unpalatable today.

Whether the demise of civilization necessarily follows the destruction of the traditional family unit as an institution, I prefer not to ponder. Suffice it to say, that question should hang heaviest on the hearts and consciences of those who by their indecisions and decisions effectively have doomed that institution.

In summary, you have information about how to fight your divorce suit. You have suggestions for opening the divorce courts to fair divorce: A National Divorce Law, and voting out or recalling judges who hand down discriminatory decisions.

You have been shown that there are alternatives —contract cohabitation and corporate marriage—to the old divorce doldrums and to divorce itself.

Whether you hate or like the ideas is not the point. The point is that divorce as it is being applied by the courts in the United States is illegal! There are alternatives.

Use them.

File your federal court suits; write to and call your congressmen and state legislators and tell them that they should get a National Divorce Law on the books and improve state laws if they want another term; and tell your local judges—possibly through a group organized for the purpose—that you expect equal treatment for men in divorces. If you do not get results, do not threaten—begin campaigns to recall or not reelect the offending judges.

It has been said through the ages that those who are governed receive the government they deserve. If the people do nothing, the best they can expect from their government is nothing.

You have information which may make it possible for men to get their rights in divorce courts as guaranteed by the Constitution of the United States of America.

So, do something!

ABOUT THE AUTHOR

Maurice R. Franks, born in 1942, received his Bachelor of Science and Juris Doctor degrees from Memphis State University. He then went to New Orleans, where he rendered "distinguished service" as Law Clerk to the Supreme Court of Louisiana. After this he served as Assistant District Attorney under New Orleans' colorful and controversial D.A. Jim Garrison.

When he is not handling cases in other parts of the country, Maurice divides his time between his office and apartment in the French Quarter of New Orleans and his house high in the mountains near Silver Cliff, Colorado. Licensed to practice before the highest courts of three states and the District of Columbia, Mr. Franks is a member of the bars of some fifteen federal courts, including the Supreme Court of the United States. He is the author of numerous scholarly articles on the law; one of his law journal articles recently was cited by the United States Court of Appeals at Philadelphia as the basis for a far-reaching decision involving class actions.

NOTES

CHAPTER VII   AVANT-GARDE VIEWS

1. J. Johnston & C. Knapp, *Sex Discrimination by Law: A Study in Judicial Perspective*, 46 N.Y.U. Law Review 675, 676 (1971).

2. "Divorced Dads Begin Campaign," United Press International dispatch, *Pueblo Chieftain*, March 7, 1975, Section A, p. 2.

3. "Marriage Rate Dips; Divorces Up," United Press International dispatch, *Pueblo Star-Journal*, February 28, 1975, Section A, p. 2.

4. D. Little, "Marriages on the Decline," *New York Times*, March 1, 1975, p. 18.

5. *Official Associated Press Almanac 1975* (Maplewood, N.J.: Hammond Almanac, Inc.), p. 229.

6. *Ibid.*, p. 224.

7. *Ibid.*

8. E. Sullivan, "The Marriage Boom, a Nationwide Report," *Redbook* magazine, February 1975, p. 173.

9. *Ibid.*

10. *Ibid.*, p. 175.

11. S. Fraiberg, "The Right to Know Love," *Redbook* magazine, February 1975, p. 128.

12. *Ibid.*

13. *Ibid.*, p. 126.

14. *Ibid.*, p. 131.

15. G. Pauley, " 'Renegotiation' Can Solve Modern Marriage Troubles," United Press International dispatch, *Pueblo Star-Journal*, March 11, 1975, Section A, p. 7.

16. *Ibid.*

CHAPTER VIII   THE FACTS

1. These tend to be the "no-fault" states, where the couple may jointly petition the court for a "dissolution of marriage."
2. 42 U.S. Code § 2000e-2.

CHAPTER IX   NO FAULT? FOUL!

1. Smith v. Goguen, 415 U.S. 566, 94 S.Ct. 1242, 39 L.Ed.2d 605 (1974).
2. Ashton v. Kentucky, 384 U.S. 195, 200, 86 S.Ct. 1407, 1410, 16 L.Ed.2d 469, 473 (1966).
3. Pheasant v. Pheasant, [1972] Q.B. (Family Div.) 202, 206, 209, 1 All E.R. 587, 589, 591, 592.
4. *Id.* at 208, [1972] 1 All E.R. at 590.
5. *Official Associated Press Almanac 1975* (Maplewood, N.J.: Hammond Almanac, Inc.), p. 228.
6. Delaware Code Annotated § 13–1505; Louisiana Revised Statutes 9:301, 9:302, Louisiana Civil Code art. 138(9); New York Domestic Relations Law §§ 170(5), 170(6).
7. *But see* McKim v. McKim, 6 Cal.3d 673, 493 P.2d 868, 871, 100 Cal.Rptr. 140 (1972), in which the Supreme Court of California said:

> Although the Legislature intended that as far as possible dissolution proceedings should be nonadversary, eliminating acrimony, it did not intend that findings of the existence of irreconcilable differences be made perfunctorily.

See also Ryan v. Ryan, 277 So.2d 266, 271 (Fla. 1973), in which the Supreme Court of Florida said:

> It is suggested that a circuit judge would hesitate to adjudicate that a marriage is *not* "irretrievably broken" under the present statute when the petitioner simply says that is the fact; that the judge becomes nothing more than a ministerial officer receiving the "irretrievably broken"

message and having so received it, being thus compelled
to drop this legislative guillotine upon the marriage, thus
excising the troublesome mate from the petitioner because
the petitioner has subjectively and unilaterally determined
that his marriage is irretrievably broken.

We do not view the matter of dissolution as being such
a simple, unilateral matter of one mate simply saying "I
want out." All of the surrounding facts and circumstances
are to be inquired into to arrive at the conclusion as to
whether or not indeed the marriage has reached the
terminal stage based upon facts which must be shown.
[Italics in original.]

8. Lawrence v. Miller, 2 N.Y. 245 (1849); Wesson &
Hunting v. Johnson, 66 N.C. 189 (1872); Bouknight v.
Epting, 11 S.C. 71 (1878); Atkinson v. Atkinson, 203
N.Y.S. 49, 207 App.Div. 660 (1924), aff'g 203 N.Y.S. 372,
121 Misc. 659 (1923); Cavanaugh v. Valentine, 41 N.Y.
S.2d 896, 181 Misc. 48 (1943). See also Irving Trust Co. v.
Day, 314 U.S. 556, 561, 62 S.Ct. 398, 401, 86 L.Ed. 452,
457 (1942)

9. 4 Wheat. 518, 4 L.Ed. 629 (1819).

10. In Dartmouth College v. Woodward, 4 Wheat 518,
693–697, 4 L.Ed. 629, 673–674 (1819), Mr. Justice
Story, concurring, said:

It is, in the first place, contended that it is not a contract within the prohibitory clause of the constitution, because that clause was never intended to apply to mere
contracts of civil institutions, such as the contract of marriage, or to grants of power to state officers, or to contracts
relative to their offices, or to grants of trust to be exercised
for purposes merely public, where the grantees take no
beneficial interest. . . .

As to the case of the contract of marriage, which the
argument supposes not to be within the reach of the prohibitory clause, because it is a matter of civil institution,
I profess not to feel the weight of the reason assigned for
the exception. . . . A general law regulating divorces from
the contract of marriage, like a law regulating remedies in
other cases of breaches of contracts, is not necessarily a
law impairing the obligation of such a contract. It may be
the only effectual mode of enforcing the obligations of the
contract on both sides. A law punishing a breach of contract, by imposing a forfeiture of the rights acquired under

it, or dissolving it because the mutual obligations were no longer observed, is in no correct sense a law impairing the obligations of the contract. Could a law, compelling a specific performance, by giving a new remedy, be justly deemed an excess of legislative power? Thus far the contract of marriage has been considered with reference to general laws regulating divorces upon breaches of that contract. But if the argument means to assert that the legislative power to dissolve such a contract, without any breach on either side, against the wishes of the parties, and without any judicial inquiry to ascertain a breach, I certainly am not prepared to admit such a power, or that its exercise would not entrench upon the prohibition of the constitution. If under the faith of existing laws a contract of marriage be duly solemnized, or a marriage settlement be made (and marriage is always in law a valuable consideration for a contract), it is not easy to perceive why a dissolution of its obligations, without any default or assent of the parties, may not as well fall within the prohibition as any other contract for a valuable consideration. A man has just as good a right to his wife as to the property acquired under a marriage contract. He has a legal right to her society and her fortune; and to divest such right without his default, and against his will, would be as flagrant a violation of the principles of justice as the confiscation of his own estate. I leave this case, however, to be settled when it shall arise.

Accord, majority opinion, *id*. at 629, 4 L.Ed. at 675, in which Chief Justice Marshall said:

The provision of the constitution never has been understood to embrace other contracts than those which respect property or some object of value, and confer rights which may be asserted in a court of justice. It never has been understood to restrict the general right of the legislature to legislate on the subject of divorces. Those acts enable some tribunal, not to impair a marriage contract, but to liberate one of the parties because it has been broken by the other. When the state legislature shall pass an act annulling all marriage contracts, or allowing either party to annul it without the consent of the other, it will be time enough to inquire whether such an act be constitutional.

See also cases cited *supra* note 8.

CHAPTER X SLAVERY!

1. U.S. Const. amend. XIII; 18 U.S. Code §§ 1581, 1583, 1584.

2. Frontiero v. Richardson, 411 U.S. 677, 93 S.Ct. 1764, 36 L.Ed.2d 583 (1973); Reed v. Reed, 404 U.S. 71, 92 S.Ct. 251, 30 L.Ed.2d 225 (1971); Taylor v. Louisiana, 95 S.Ct. 692, 42 L.Ed.2d 690 (1975); 42 U.S. Code § 2000e-2.

3. Plessy v. Ferguson, 163 U.S. 537, 542, 16 S.Ct. 1138, 1140, 41 L.Ed. 256, 257 (1896).

4. 42 U.S. Code § 2000e-2.

5. In re Lewis, 114 F. 963, 967 (N.D. Fla. 1902). In Peonage Cases, 123 F. 671, 673–674 (M.D. Ala. 1903), it is said:

Peonage was not slavery, as it formerly existed in this country. The peon was not a slave. He was a freeman, with political as well as civil rights. He entered into the relation from choice, as the result of mutual contract. The relation was not confined to any race. The child of a peon did not become a peon, and the father could not contract away the services of his minor child, except in rare cases. The peon, male or female, agreed with the master upon the nature of the service, the length of its duration, and compensation.

6. U.S. Const. art. VI; Hamm v. City of Rock Hill, 379 U.S. 306, 85 S.Ct. 384, 13 L.Ed.2d 300 (1964).

7. 42 U.S. Code § 1994.

8. U.S. Const. amend. XIII.

9. Bailey v. Alabama, 219 U.S. 219, 240–241, 31 S.Ct. 146, 151, 55 L.Ed. 191, 201 (1911).

10. In Clyatt v. United States, 197 U.S. 207, 215, 25 S.Ct. 429, 430, 49 L.Ed. 726, 729 (1905), the Supreme Court said:

Peonage is sometimes classified as voluntary or involuntary, but this implies simply a difference in the mode of origin, but none in the character of the servitude. The one exists where the debtor voluntarily contracts to enter the service of his creditor. The other is forced upon the debtor by some provision of law. But peonage, however created, is compulsory service, involuntary servitude. The peon can release himself therefrom, it is true, by the payment of the debt, but otherwise the service is enforced.

And in Peonage Cases, 136 F. 707, 708–709 (D. Ark. 1905), the United States District Court for the District of Arkansas said:

It is wholly immaterial whether the contract whereby the laborer is to work out an indebtedness due from him to the employer is entered into voluntarily or not. The laws of the United States declare all such contracts null and void, and they cannot be enforced. It is immaterial whether such a contract is made in consideration of a pre-existing indebtedness, or for a loan made at the time the contract is made. The law prohibits them, and, if made, declares the contract null and void; and any person who holds, arrests, returns, or causes to be held, arrested, or returned, or in any manner aids in the arrest or return of, any person to a condition of peonage, is, as I stated before, guilty of an offense against the laws of the United States, and subject to indictment by a grand jury of the district in which the acts are committed.

11. Taylor v. Georgia, 315 U.S. 25, 62 S.Ct. 415, 86 L.Ed. 615 (1942).

12. In Pollock v. Williams, 322 U.S. 4, 18, 64 S.Ct. 792, 799, 88 L.Ed. 1095, 1104 (1944), the Supreme Court said:

Whatever of social value there may be, and of course it is great, in enforcing contracts and collection of debts, Congress has put it beyond debate that no indebtedness warrants a suspension of the right to be free from compulsory service. This congressional policy means that no state can make the quitting of work any component of a crime, or make criminal sanctions available for holding unwilling persons to labor. The federal statutory test is a practical inquiry into the utilization of an act as well as its mere form and terms.

13. *Id.*

14. In Clyatt v. United States, *supra* note 10, at 216, 25 S.Ct. at 430, 49 L.Ed. at 729, the Supreme Court said:

We need not stop to consider any possible limits or exceptional cases, such as the service of a sailor, *Robertson* v. *Baldwin*, 165 U.S. 275, or the obligations of a child to its parents, or of an apprentice to his master, or the power of the legislature to make unlawful and punish criminally an abandonment by an employé of his post of labor in any extreme cases.

And in Peonage Cases, *supra* note 5, at 681, the United States District Court for the Middle District of Alabama said:

Instances where such compulsory service may be enforced arise in the case of parent and child, master and apprentice, as to certain services to be rendered the government, as in the army and navy, and also where the state exacts public duties of the citizen, such as service in the militia, working of the public roads, and the like.

15. In the case of Richardson, v. Richardson, 112 F.2d 19 (D.C. Cir. 1940), in an opinion written by Mr. Justice Vinson while still an associate justice on the United States Court of Appeals for the District of Columbia Circuit, before his appointment to the Supreme Court as Chief Justice of the United States, the United States Court of Appeals for the District of Columbia Circuit ruled that the interest of the wife in jointly held property is conditioned on her faithful performance of the marriage vows. The court upheld the decision of the United States District Court for the District of Columbia divesting the wife of her interest in the real estate and in a bank account.

CHAPTER XI THE EQUAL-RIGHTS AMENDMENT

1. 28 U.S. Code § 1343 provides:

The district courts shall have original jurisdiction of any civil action authorized by law to be commenced by any person:

....

(3) To redress the deprivation, under color of any State law, statute, ordinance, regulation, custom or usage, of any right, privilege or immunity secured by the Consti-

tution of the United States or by any Act of Congress providing for equal rights of citizens or of all persons within the jurisdiction of the United States. . . .

2. Bradwell v. Illinois, 83 U.S. (16 Wall.) 130, 21 L.Ed. 442 (1873); Minor v. Happersett, 88 U.S. (21 Wall.) 162, 22 L.Ed. 627 (1874); Muller v. Oregon, 208 U.S. 412, 28 S.Ct. 324, 52 L.Ed. 551 (1908); Goesaert v. Clary 335 U.S. 464, 69 S.Ct. 198, 93 L.Ed. 163 (1948); Hoyt v. Florida, 368 U.S. 57, 82 S.Ct. 159, 7 L.Ed.2d 118 (1961).

3. Sail'er Inn, Inc. v. Kirby, 5 Cal.3d 1, 18, 485 P.2d 529, 540, 95 Cal.Rptr. 329, 340 (1971).

4. 404 U.S. 71, 92 S.Ct. 251, 30 L.Ed.2d 225 (1971).

5. 411 U.S. 677, 93 S.Ct. 1764, 36 L.Ed.2d 583 (1973).

6. Frontiero v. Richardson, 411 U.S. 677, 682, 93 S.Ct. 1764, 1768, 36 L.Ed.2d 583, 589 (1973).

7. 414 U.S. 973, 94 S.Ct. 1734, 40 L.Ed.2d 189 (1974). Kahn v. Shevin may be distinguished from Reed v. Reed, 404 U.S. 71, 92 S.Ct. 251, 30 L.Ed.2d 225 (1971), and from Frontiero v. Richardson, *supra* note 6, on the same basis that, say, Walz v. Tax Commission, 397 U.S. 664, 90 S.Ct. 1409, 25 L.Ed.2d 697 (1970), may be distinguished from Epperson v. Arkansas, 393 U.S. 97, 89 S.Ct. 266, 21 L.Ed.2d 228 (1968), and from Engel v. Vitale, 370 U.S. 421, 82 S.Ct. 1261, 8 L.Ed.2d 601 (1962). Studying the cases, the principle of law emerges: state tax exemptions are *sui generis*. Thus, Walz v. Tax Commission in no way overrules Epperson v. Arkansas or Engel v. Vitale. Likewise, Kahn v. Shevin in no way overrules Reed v. Reed or Frontiero v. Richardson.

8. Stanton v. Stanton, 419 U.S. 893, 95 S.Ct. 170, 42 L.Ed.2d 137 (1974). Quaere: Is the Court agreeing to reexamine its holding in Kahn v. Shevin, 414 U.S. 973, 94 S.Ct. 1734, 40 L.Ed.2d 189 (1974)?

9. Taylor v. Louisiana, 95 S.Ct. 692, 42 L.Ed.2d 690 (1975).

10. Daniel v. Louisiana, 95 S.Ct. 704, 42 L.Ed.2d 790 (1975).

11. D. Sassower, *Women and the Judiciary: Undoing "The Law of the Creator,"* 80 Case & Comment 30 (Jan.–Feb. 1975).

12. S.J. Res. 8, 92nd Cong. 1st Sess. (1971).

13. U.S. Const. art. VI; Hamm v. City of Rock Hill, 379 U.S. 306, 85 S.Ct. 384, 13 L.Ed.2d 300 (1964).

14. In J. Johnston & C. Knapp, *Sex Discrimination by Law: A Study in Judicial Perspective,* 46 N.Y.U. Law Review 675, 747 (1971), it is said:

> Another aspect of the judicial role is the responsibility to be *ahead* of other men. Judges are not entitled to the luxury of shielding themselves behind public opinion or community attitudes, however strongly held those may be. The judiciary thus cannot shift responsibility to the legislatures, the press, women's liberation activists or anyone else. A judge whose opinions on important questions of public policy reflect nothing more than his private estimate of public majority opinion is engaging in journalism, not jurisprudence. [Italics in original.]

CHAPTER XII SOME TRAILBLAZING

1. Ashby v. White, 2 Ld. Raym. 938, 953 (1703).

CHAPTER XIII WHAT

1. England v. Louisiana State Board of Medical Examiners, 375 U.S. 413, 84 S.Ct. 461, 11 L.Ed.2d 440 (1964).

2. In Franks v. Wilson, 369 F.Supp. 304, 308 (D. Colo, 1973), *stay denied,* 414 U.S. 1123, 94 S.Ct. 859, 38 L.Ed.2d 749 (1974), *appeal dismissed for want of jurisdiction,* 415 U.S. 986, 94 S.Ct. 1583, 39 L.Ed.2d 884 (1974) (Mr. Justice Douglas dissents from the dismissal of the appeal), *rehearing denied,* 416 U.S. 975, 94 S.Ct. 2004, 40 L.Ed.2d 565 (1974), a three-judge panel of the United States District Court for the District of Colorado stayed proceedings "to permit plaintiff to obtain from the state courts of Colorado, a determination of whether or not the pre-nuptial agreement is enforceable in the proceeding now pending in the state court." *See also* Harris County Commissioners Court v. Moore, 95 S.Ct. 870 (1975).

3. U.S. Const. amend I. In California Motor Transport

Co. v. Trucking Unlimited, 404 U.S. 508, 510, 92 S.Ct. 609, 612, 30 L.Ed.2d 642, 646 (1972), the Supreme Court, speaking through Mr. Justice Douglas, said:

> Certainly the right to petition extends to all departments of the Government. The right of access to the courts is indeed but one aspect of the right of petition.

4. 28 U.S. Code § 1446(b) provides:

> The petition for removal of a civil action or proceeding shall be filed within thirty days after the receipt by the defendant, through service or otherwise, of a copy of the initial pleading setting forth the claim for relief upon which such action or proceeding is based, or within thirty days after the service of summons upon the defendant if such initial pleading has then been filed in court and is not required to be served on the defendant, whichever period is shorter.

5. Once the case is removed, it is no longer pending in state court. 28 U.S. Code § 1446(e). Even if the case has been removed improvidently, it is reversible error for the state court to proceed until such time as the case is remanded. Echevarria v. Silberglitt, 441 F.2d 225 (2d Cir. 1971); Schuchman v. State, 250 Ind. 408, 236 N.E.2d 830 (1968). Thus, where no award of temporary maintenance has been made by the state court prior to removal, the state court is powerless to make such an award after removal until such time as the case is remanded. As applied to interlocutory orders in civil cases, see Adair Pipeline Co. v. Pipeliners Local 798, 325 F.2d 206 (5th Cir. 1963). After remand, the state court may award maintenance prospectively only in most states. This would seem especially true where the state court lacked jurisdiction over the parties prior to remand.

6. See Chapter XVI of this book.

CHAPTER XIV   HOW

1. 28 U.S. Code § 2281 provides:

An interlocutory or permanent injunction restraining the
enforcement, operation or execution of any State statute
by restraining the action of any officer of such State in the
enforcement or execution of such statute or of an order
made by an administrative board or commission acting
under State statutes, shall not be granted by any district
court or judge thereof upon the ground of the unconstitutionality of such statute unless the application therefor is
heard and determined by a district court composed of three
judges under section 2284 of this title.

2. Geisinger v. Voss, 352 F.Supp. 104 (E.D. Wis.
1972); Wymelenberg v. Syman, 328 F.Supp. 1353 (E.D.
Wis. 1971); McCay v. State of South Dakota, 366 F.Supp.
1244 (D. S.Dak. 1973).
3. 28 U.S. Code § 2284(1); Geisinger v. Voss, *supra*
note 2.
4. Geisinger v. Voss, *supra* note 2; Franks v. Wilson,
369 F.Supp. 304 (D. Colo. 1973), *stay denied*, 414 U.S.
1123, 94 S.Ct. 859, 38 L.Ed.2d 749 (1974), *appeal dismissed for want of jurisdiction*, 415 U.S. 986, 94 S.Ct.
1583, 39 L.Ed.2d 884 (1974) (Mr. Justice Douglas dissents from the dismissal of the appeal), *rehearing denied*,
416 U.S. 975, 94 S.Ct. 2004, 40 L.Ed.2d 565 (1974).
5. 28 U.S. Code § 2284(1).
6. 28 U.S. Code § 1253. But watch out! Gonzales v.
Automatic Employees Credit Union, 95 S.Ct. 289, 42
L.Ed.2d 249 (1974); Mitchell v. Donovan, 398 U.S. 427,
90 S.Ct. 1763, 26 L.Ed.2d 378 (1970); Gunn v. University Committee to End the War in Vietnam, 399 U.S.
383, 90 S.Ct. 2013, 26 L.Ed.2d 684 (1970); Turner v. City
of Memphis, 369 U.S. 350, 82 S.Ct. 805, 7 L.Ed.2d 762
(1962); Bailey v. Patterson, 369 U.S. 31, 82 S.Ct. 549,
7 L.Ed.2d 512 (1962). *See also* Hagans v. Levine, 415
U.S. 528, 94 S.Ct. 1372, 39 L.Ed.2d 577 (1974). The
careful attorney will perfect dual appeals, one to the Supreme Court and one to the Court of Appeals. Ammer-

man, *Three Judge Courts: See How They Run!* 52 F.R.D. 293, 302–303 (1971).

7. Carter v. Stanton, 405 U.S. 669, 92 S.Ct. 1232, 31 L.Ed.2d 569 (1972); Monroe v. Pape, 365 U.S. 167, 81 S.Ct. 473, 5 L.Ed.2d 492 (1961); *cf.* Zwickler v. Koota, 389 U.S. 241, 254, 88 S.Ct. 391, 399, 19 L.Ed.2d 444, 454 (1967); Bailey v. Patterson, *supra* note 6. *See also* Kusper v. Pontikes, 414 U.S. 51, 94 S.Ct. 303, 38 L.Ed.2d 260 (1973).

8. 42 U.S. Code § 1983.

9. See Chapters IX, X, and XI of this book.

10. Unconstitutionality of the law *as applied* is sufficient to warrant convening a three-judge court. Steffel v. Thompson, 415 U.S. 452, 94 S.Ct. 1209, 39 L.Ed.2d 505 (1974); Turner v. Fouche, 396 U.S. 346, 90 S.Ct. 532, 24 L.Ed.2d 567 (1970). As specifically applied to divorce cases, see Geisinger v. Voss, *supra* note 2.

11. U.S. Const. amend. XIV; 16 Am.Jur.2d *Constitutional Law* § 540.

12. Exhaustion of state remedies is not necessary. See cases cited *supra* note 7.

13. Wood v. Strickland, 95 S.Ct. 992 (1975). As specifically applied to divorce cases, see Larsen v. Gallogly, 361 F.Supp. 305, 310–311 (D. R.I. 1973), *vacated and remanded with instructions to dismiss as moot,* 95 S.Ct. 819, 42 L.Ed.2d 831 (1975), in which the United States District Court for the District of Rhode Island said: "The doctrine of judicial immunity does not, however, prevent the grant of injunctive relief against a judge in a proper case." *See also* Mon Chi Hueng Au v. Lum, 360 F.Supp. 219 (D. Haw. 1973).

14. 28 U.S. Code § 2281; Geisinger v. Voss, *supra* note 2.

15. See cases cited *supra* note 10.

16. England v. Louisiana State Board of Medical Examiners, 375 U.S. 413, 84 S.Ct. 461, 11 L.Ed.2d 440 (1964).

17. *Id.*

18. In England v. Louisiana State Board of Medical Examiners, *supra* note 16, at 423 n. 13, 84 S.Ct. at 468, 11 L.Ed.2d at 449, the Supreme Court said:

Once issue has been joined in the federal court, no party
is entitled to insist, over another's objection, upon a binding state court determination of the federal question. Thus,
while a plaintiff who unreservedly litigates his federal
claims in the state courts may thereby elect to forgo his
own right to return to the District Court, he cannot impair
the corresponding right of the defendant.

19. 396 S.W.2d 855 (Tex. 1965). *See also* Harris
County Commissioners Court v. Moore, 95 S.Ct. 870, 877
n. 14 (1975).
20. Johnson v. Rockefeller, 58 F.R.D. 42 (S.D.N.Y.
1973); *see* Dunn v. Blumstein, 405 U.S. 330, 92 S.Ct. 995,
31 L.Ed.2d 274 (1972); Shiffman v. Askew, 359 F.Supp.
1225 (M.D. Fla. 1973).
21. 28 U.S. Code § 2284(2).
22. Doe v. Scott, 321 F.Supp. 1385 (N.D. Ill. 1971);
see Shiffman v. Askew, *supra* note 20; Doe v. Bolton, 410
U.S. 179, 93 S.Ct. 739, 35 L.Ed.2d 201 (1973); Fuentes
v. Shevin, 407 U.S. 67, 92 S.Ct. 1983, 32 L.Ed.2d 556
(1973).
23. In Johnson v. University of Pittsburgh, 359 F.Supp.
1002, 1008 (W.D. Pa. 1973), the United States District
Court for the Western District of Pennsylvania said:

We agree that the statistics and other evidence of discrimination showing the imbalance of men and women
with tenure in the School of Medicine and the Department
of Biochemistry in particular make out a prima facie case
which imposes upon the defendant the duty to go forward
with rebutting evidence.

Accord, Penn v. Eubanks, 360 F.Supp. 699, 703 (M.D.
Ala. 1973); Associated General Contractors of Massachusetts, Inc. v. Altshuler, 361 F.Supp. 1293 (D. Mass. 1973),
aff'd, 490 F.2d 9 (1st Cir. 1973), *cert. denied*, 416 U.S.
957, 94 S.Ct. 1971, 40 L.Ed.2d 307 (1974).
24. 42 U.S. Code § 2000e-2; Weeks v. Southern Bell
Telephone and Telegraph Company, 408 F.2d 228 (5th
Cir. 1969); Schaeffer v. San Diego Yellow Cabs, Inc., 462
F.2d 1002 (9th Cir. 1972); Burns v. Rohr Corporation,
346 F.Supp. 994 (S.D. Cal. 1972); Wilson v. Sibley
Memorial Hospital, 340 F.Supp. 686 (D. D.C. 1972), *rev'd*

on other grounds, 488 F.2d 1338 (D.C. Cir. 1973); LeBlanc v. Southern Bell Telephone and Telegraph Company, 333 F.Supp. 602 (E.D. La. 1971), *aff'd*, 460 F.2d 1228 (5th Cir. 1972), *cert. denied*, 409 U.S. 990, 93 S.Ct. 320, 34 L.Ed.2d 257 (1972).

25. Frontiero v. Richardson, 411 U.S. 677, 93 S.Ct. 1764, 36 L.Ed.2d 583 (1973).

26. Geisinger v. Voss, *supra* note 2. *See also* Patterson v. Patterson, 381 F.Supp. 1029 (D. Colo. 1974).

27. State ex rel. Watts v. Watts, 350 N.Y.S.2d 285 (1973).

28. Conway v. Dana, 318 A.2d 324, 326 (Pa. 1974).

29. In his dissenting opinion in Clay v. Sun Insurance Office Limited, 363 U.S. 207, 228, 80 S.Ct. 1222, 1234, 4 L.Ed.2d 1170, 1185 (1960), Mr. Justice Douglas said:

> The situations where a federal court might await decision in a state court or even remand the parties to it should be the exception not the rule. Only prejudice against diversity jurisdiction can explain the avoidance of the simple constitutional question that is presented here and the remittance of the parties to state courts to begin the litigation anew. Some litigants have long purses. Many, however, can hardly afford one lawsuit, let alone two. Shuttling the parties between state and federal tribunals is a sure way of defeating the ends of justice. The pursuit of justice is not an academic exercise. There are no foundations to finance the resolution of nice state law questions involved in federal court litigation.

30. In the American Law Institute's Study of the Division of Jurisdiction between State and Federal Courts, Tentative Draft No. 3 (April 15, 1965), Commentary, § 1361, it is said:

> The Leiter Minerals litigation remains unresolved, Leiter Minerals, Inc. v. United States, 329 F.2d 85 (5th Cir. 1964), more than eleven years after it was commenced and seven years after abstention was ordered. Leiter Minerals, Inc. v. United States, 352 U.S. 220 [77 S.Ct. 287, 1 L.Ed.2d 267] (1957).

CHAPTER XV   MORE HOW

1. 28 U.S. Code § 1446(b).
2. 381 F.Supp. 1029 (D. Colo. 1974).
3. 350 N.Y.S.2d 285 (1973).
4. 318 A.2d 324 (Pa. 1974).
5. Patterson v. Patterson, 381 F.Supp. 1029 (D. Colo. 1974).
6. The procedure for removal is set forth in 28 U.S. Code § 1446, which provides in part:

(a) A defendant or defendants desiring to remove any civil action or criminal prosecution from a State court shall file in the district court of the United States for the district and division within which such action is pending a verified petition containing a short and plain statement of the facts which entitle him or them to removal together with a copy of all process, pleadings and orders served upon him or them in such action.

....

(d) Each petition for removal in a civil action or proceeding, except a petition in behalf of the United States, shall be accompanied by a bond with good and sufficient surety conditioned that the defendant or defendants will pay all costs and disbursements incurred by reason of the removal proceedings should it be determined that the case was not removable or was improperly removed.

7. 28 U.S. Code § 1446(e).
8. Echevarria v. Silberglitt, 441 F.2d 225 (2d Cir. 1971); Schuchman v. State, 250 Ind. 408, 236 N.E.2d 830 (1968).
9. As applied to interlocutory orders in civil cases, see Adair Pipeline Co. v. Pipeliners Local 798, 325 F.2d 206 (5th Cir. 1963).
10. *Supra* notes 8 and 9.
11. *See* Wade v. Bethesda Hospital, 337 F.Supp. 671, *motion denied,* 356 F.Supp. 380 (S.D. Ohio 1971).
12. 28 U.S. Code § 1443(1).
13. 32 Am.Jur.2d *Federal Practice and Procedure* § 475, at 1024; Peacock v. Greenwood, 347 F.2d 679 (5th Cir.),

rev'd on other grounds, 384 U.S. 808, 86 S.Ct. 1800, 16 L.Ed.2d 944 (1966).

14. Frontiero v. Richardson, 411 U.S. 677, 93 S.Ct. 1764, 36 L.Ed.2d 583 (1973). *See also* Reed v. Reed, 404 U.S. 71, 92 S.Ct. 251, 30 L.Ed.2d 225 (1971); Taylor v. Louisiana, 95 S.Ct. 692, 42 L.Ed.2d 690 (1975).

15. Warren v. United States, 340 U.S. 523, 71 S.Ct. 432, 95 L.Ed. 503 (1951).

16. *Id.* at 526, 71 S.Ct. at 434, 95 L.Ed. at 508.

17. Jackson v. City of Vicksburg, 361 F.2d 473 (5th Cir. 1966); Walker v. State of Georgia, 417 F.2d 511 (5th Cir. 1969); Robinson v. State of Florida, 345 F.2d 133 (5th Cir. 1965); Whatley v. City of Vidalia, 399 F.2d 521 (5th Cir. 1968); Calhoun v. City of Meridian, 355 F.2d 209 (5th Cir. 1966). *See also* Thompson v. Brown, 434 F.2d 1092 (5th Cir. 1969).

18. Associated General Contractors of Massachusetts, Inc., v. Altshuler, 361 F.Supp. 1293 (D. Mass. 1973), *aff'd,* 490 F.2d 9 (1st Cir. 1973), *cert. denied,* 416 U.S. 957, 94 S.Ct. 1971, 40 L.Ed.2d 307 (1974); Penn v. Eubanks, 360 F.Supp. 699, 703 (M.D. Ala. 1973); Johnson v. University of Pittsburgh, 359 F.Supp. 1002, 1008 (W.D. Pa. 1973).

19. Federal Rules of Civil Procedure 36(a); United States v. Wiman, 304 F.2d 53 (5th Cir. 1962), *cert. denied,* 372 U.S. 915, 83 S.Ct. 717, 9 L.Ed.2d 722 (1963); Jackson v. Riley Stoker Corporation, 57 F.R.D. 120 (E.D. Pa. 1972); Balistrieri v. Holtzman, 55 F.R.D. 470, 472–473 (E.D. Wis. 1972).

20. 415 U.S. 423, 94 S.Ct. 1113, 39 L.Ed.2d 435 (1974).

21. Wabash W.R. Co. v. Brow, 164 U.S. 271, 17 S.Ct. 126, 41 L.Ed. 431 (1896).

22. For example, see M. Franks, *Federal Remedies for Sexual Discrimination Against Male Divorce Litigants,* 4 Colorado Lawyer 231 (1975).

23. Fuentes v. Shevin, 407 U.S. 67, 92 S.Ct. 1983, 32 L.Ed.2d 556 (1972). As specifically applied to divorce cases, see Geisinger v. Voss, 352 F.Supp. 104 (E.D. Wis. 1972).

24. United States v. Thirty Seven Photographs, 402 U.S. 363, 367, 91 S.Ct. 1400, 1403, 28 L.Ed.2d 822, 828–829

NOTES 159

(1971); Near v. Minnesota, 283 U.S. 697, 713–716, 51 S.Ct. 625, 630–631, 75 L.Ed. 1357, 1366–1367 (1931).

25. In Granny Goose Foods, Inc. v. Brotherhood of Teamsters, 415 U.S. 423, 437, 439–440, 94 S.Ct. 1113, 1123, 1124, 39 L.Ed.2d 435, 449, 451 (1974), the Supreme Court said:

> More importantly, once a case has been removed to federal court, it is settled that federal rather than state law governs the future course of proceedings, notwithstanding state court orders issued prior to removal.
>
> ....
>
> An *ex parte* temporary restraining order issued by a state court prior to removal remains in force after removal no longer than it would have remained in effect under state law, but in no event does the order remain in force longer than the time limitations imposed by Rule 65(b), measured from the date of removal.

26. An order of remand entered in a case removed pursuant to 28 U.S. Code § 1443 is appealable to the United States Court of Appeals. 28 U.S. Code § 1447(d) provides:

> An order remanding a case to the State court from which it was removed is not reviewable on appeal or otherwise, except that an order remanding a case to the State court from which it was removed pursuant to section 1443 of this title shall be reviewable by appeal or otherwise.

27. In the hypothetical case of Diane and Talbot Jones (Chapter VI), Mrs. Jones was not supporting her husband in the manner to which he had become accustomed. Equal employment opportunity carries with it equal support responsibility. *See* Conway v. Dana, 318 A.2d 324 (Pa. 1974). If anything, the court should order *her* to pay *him* alimony and child support. Any other decree would reflect a sexist double standard.

28. Georgia v. Rachel, 384 U.S. 780, 86 S.Ct. 1783, 16 L.Ed.2d 925 (1966); Greenwood v. Peacock, 384 U.S. 808, 86 S.Ct. 1800, 16 L.Ed.2d 944 (1966). As specifically applied to domestic relations cases, see State of Ohio v. Denman, 462 F.2d 1292 (6th Cir. 1972); Penn-

sylvania ex rel. Rothenberg v. Beers, 450 F.2d 783 (3d Cir. 1971).

29. 28 U.S. Code § 1443.

30. Harper v. Virginia Board of Elections, 383 U.S. 663, 669, 86 S.Ct. 1079, 1083, 16 L.Ed.2d 169, 174, (1966).

31. See Sail'er Inn, Inc. v. Kirby, 5 Cal.3d 1, 18, 485 P.2d 529, 540, 95 Cal.Rptr. 329, 340 (1971).

32. Supra note 26.

33. Why not try a removal based on 28 U.S. Code § 1441(b)? See footnote 13 to the majority opinion in England v. Louisiana State Board of Medical Examiners, 375 U.S. 413, 423 n. 13, 84 S.Ct. 461, 468, 11 L.Ed.2d 440, 449 (1964), in which the Supreme Court said:

> The reservation may be made by any party to the litigation. Usually the plaintiff will have made the original choice to litigate in the federal court, but the defendant also, by virtue of the removal jurisdiction, 28 U.S.C. § 1441(b), has a right to litigate the federal question there.

CHAPTER XVI   SOME FACTS AND FIGURES

1. "Marriage Rate Dips; Divorces Up," United Press International dispatch, *Pueblo Star-Journal*, February 28, 1975, Section A, p. 2.

2. Office of the State Courts Administrator (Florida), *Florida Judicial System Statistical Report 1973*, p. 57.

3. Office of the Administrative Judge of the New York State Courts.

4. Illinois Department of Public Health, *Vital Statistics Special Report No. 53* (July 1974), p. 1.

5. Office of the Judicial Administrator (Colorado), *Domestic Relations Terminations for the State—1972* (1973).

6. *Ibid.*

7. See People. v. Elliott, 525 P.2d 457 (Colo. 1974), in which the Supreme Court of Colorado, *en banc,* saw nothing wrong with the former Colorado statute that made it a felony for men (but not for women) to fail to support their minor children. See also Murphy v. Murphy, 206 S.E.2d 458 (Ga. 1974). Both courts mistakenly rely on

Kahn v. Shevin, 414 U.S. 973, 94 S.Ct. 1734, 40 L.Ed.2d 189 (1974). As of this writing, a petition for a writ of certiorari has been filed with the Supreme Court of the United States in the *Murphy* case, but has not been acted upon by the high Court. This writer has information that the Supreme Court is withholding action either granting or denying certiorari in the *Murphy* case pending the handing down of an opinion in Stanton v. Stanton, *probable jurisdiction noted,* 419 U.S. 893, 95 S.Ct. 170, 42 L.Ed.2d 137 (1974). As soon as *Stanton* is decided, the Supreme Court will either grant or deny a writ of certiorari in *Murphy*.

8. California Department of Public Health, *Marriage and Divorce in California—1966–1969* (Calif. 1971), p. 26.

9. California Department of Health, *Vital Statistics— Marriages and Marriage Dissolutions—January–December 1973* (May 1974), p. 1.

10. California Department of Public Health, *Marriage and Divorce in California—1966–1969* (Calif. 1971), p. 29.

11. California Department of Public Health, *Divorce in California—1966* (Calif. 1967), pp. 17–18.

12. *Ibid.,* p. 34.

13. *Ibid.*

14. 24 Am.Jur.2d *Divorce and Separation* §§ 645, 690; Annot., Alimony—Effect of Remarriage, 48 A.L.R.2d 270 (1956).

15. *See, e.g.,* Murphy v. Murphy, *supra* note 7.

16. Missouri Center for Health Statistics, *Missouri Vital Statistics 1973* (1974), p. 148.

17. *Ibid.*

18. *Ibid.*

19. *Ibid.*

20. *Ibid.* p. 149.

21. *Ibid.*

22. *Ibid.*

23. Johnson v. University of Pittsburgh, 359 F.Supp. 1002, 1008 (W.D. Pa. 1973); Penn v. Eubanks, 360 F.Supp. 699, 703 (M.D. Ala. 1973); Associated General Contractors of Massachusetts, Inc. v. Altshuler, 361 F.Supp.

1293 (D. Mass. 1973), *aff'd*, 490 F.2d 9 (1st Cir. 1973), *cert. denied*, 416 U.S. 957, 94 S.Ct. 1971, 40 L.Ed.2d 307 (1974).

CHAPTER XVII CHILD SUPPORT—YES, BUT . . .

1. 42 U.S. Code § 2000e-2.
2. Conway v. Dana, 318 A.2d 324 (Pa. 1974).
3. *Id.* at 326.
4. U.S. Const. amend. XIII; 42 U.S. Code § 1994.
5. Clyatt v. United States, 197 U.S. 207, 216, 25 S.Ct. 429, 430, 49 L.Ed. 726, 729 (1905); Peonage Cases, 123 F. 671, 681 (M.D. Ala. 1903).
6. But be mindful of the dangers of unreservedly litigating federal issues in state court. England v. Louisiana State Board of Medical Examiners, 375 U.S. 413, 84 S.Ct. 461, 11 L.Ed.2d 440 (1964).
7. Ventresco v. Bushey, 159 Me. 241, 191 A.2d 104 (1963); Vasquez v. Esquibel, 141 Colo. 5, 346 P.2d 293 (1959); Loudon v. Loudon, 114 N.J. Eq. 242, 168 A. 840 (1933); Yerian v. Brinker, 33 Ohio L. Abs. 591, 35 N.E. 2d 878 (1941).
8. 10 Am.Jur.2d *Bastards* § 23.
9. R. Ratimorszky, *Blood Tests in Paternity Cases*, 19 Cleveland State L. Rev. 491 (1970); 10 Am.Jur.2d *Bastards* § 32.
10. Comment, *California's Conclusive Presumption of Legitimacy—Its Legal Effect and Its Questionable Constitutionality*, 35 Southern Calif. L. Rev. 437, 467–474 (1962).

CHAPTER XVIII ENDING ALIMONY?

1. Weeks v. Southern Bell Telephone and Telegraph Company, 408 F.2d 228, 236 (5th Cir. 1969).
2. Schaeffer v. San Diego Yellow Cabs, Inc., 462 F.2d 1002 (9th Cir. 1972).
3. 346 F.Supp. 994 (S.D. Cal. 1972).
4. 340 F.Supp. 686 (D. D.C. 1972), *rev'd on other grounds*, 488 F.2d 1338 (D.C. Cir. 1973).

5. 333 F.Supp. 602 (E.D. La. 1971), *aff'd*, 460 F.2d 1228 (5th Cir. 1972), *cert. denied*, 409 U.S. 990, 93 S.Ct. 320, 34 L.Ed.2d 257 (1972).

6. LeBlanc v. Southern Bell Telephone and Telegraph Company, 333 F.Supp. 602, 603 hn. 6 (E.D. La. 1971), *aff'd*, 460 F.2d 1228 (5th Cir. 1972), *cert. denied*, 409 U.S. 990, 93 S.Ct. 320, 34 L.Ed.2d 257 (1972).

7. Conway v. Dana, 318 A.2d 324 (Pa. 1974).

8. *Id. See also* State ex rel. Watts v. Watts, 350 N.Y.S.2d 285 (1973).

9. Public Law 93–495, Title V, § 503, Oct. 28, 1974, 88 Stat. 1521.

10. 15 U.S. Code § 1691. *See also* 12 U.S. Code § 1735f-5.

11. *But see* Kohler v. Ogilvie, 53 F.R.D. 98 (N.D. Ill. 1971), *aff'd*, 405 U.S. 906, 92 S.Ct. 938, 30 L.Ed.2d 777 (1972).

12. Richardson v. Richardson, 112 F.2d 19 (D.C. Cir. 1940).

CHAPTER XIX   YES, THEY'RE MARRIED

1. 391 U.S. 68, 88 S.Ct. 1509, 20 L.Ed.2d 436 (1968).

2. 391 U.S. 73, 88 S.Ct. 1515, 20 L.Ed.2d 441 (1968).

3. Levy v. Louisiana, 391 U.S. 68, 88 S.Ct. 1509, 20 L.Ed.2d 436 (1968).

4. Glona v. American Guarantee and Liability Insurance Company, 391 U.S. 73, 88 S.Ct. 1515, 20 L.Ed.2d 441 (1968).

5. 169 Ohio St. 276, 159 N.E.2d 430 (1959).

6. 60 N.M. 432, 292 P.2d 115 (1956).

7. Hunt v. Hunt, 169 Ohio St. 276, 159 N.E.2d 430, 439 (1959); Kuert v. Kuert, 60 N.M. 432, 292 P.2d 115, 120 (1956).

8. Hunt v. Hunt, *supra* note 7, 159 N.E.2d at 439.

9. 36 Ohio App.2d 208, 304 N.E.2d 411 (1973).

10. Fahrer v. Fahrer, 36 Ohio App.2d 208, 304, N.E.2d 411, 413 (1973).

11. *See* 52 Am.Jur.2d *Marriage* §§ 42–61.

12. 24 Am.Jur.2d *Divorce and Separation* §§ 645, 690;

Annot., Alimony—Effect of Remarriage, 48 A.L.R.2d 270 (1956).

13. *Id.*

14. *Id.*

15. As of this writing, the strongest is Fahrer v. Fahrer, *supra* note 10.

16. Kuert v. Kuert, *supra* note 7, 292 P.2d at 120.

17. Levy v. Louisiana, *supra* note 3; Glona v. American Guarantee and Liability Insurance Company, *supra* note 4.

CHAPTER XX FOR THE NEXT TIME

1. Requirements as to form and wording are highly technical and vary greatly from state to state. See, *e.g.*, Louisiana Civil Code art. 2328. For a painful example of the invalidity of a particular do-it-yourself marriage contract, see Irving Trust Co. v. Day, 314 U.S. 556, 62 S.Ct. 398, 86 L.Ed. 452 (1942).

2. Note, *Love Means Never Having to Say You're Suing*, 60 A.B.A.J. 628 (May 1974).

CHAPTER XXI SO, DO SOMETHING!

1. *Webster's Guide to American History* (Springfield, Mass.: G. & C. Merriam Co.), p. 1313.

2. *Ibid.*

3. *Ibid.*, p. 163.

4. People v. Elliott, 525 P.2d 457 (Colo. 1974).

5. According to the *Official Associated Press Almanac 1975* (Maplewood, N.J.: Hammond Almanac, Inc.), p. 224, U.S. Bureau of the Census figures show that in 1973 there were 2.7 million divorced men and 4 million (50% more) divorced women in the United States. Even taking into account the longevity differences between men and women, the statistics seem to indicate that more divorced men remarry than divorced women.

Index

ABOUT THE AUTHOR

Maurice R. Franks, born in 1942, received his Bachelor of Science and Juris Doctor degrees from Memphis State University. He then went to New Orleans, where he rendered "distinguished service" as Law Clerk to the Supreme Court of Louisiana. After this he served as Assistant District Attorney under New Orleans' colorful and controversial D.A. Jim Garrison.

When he is not handling cases in other parts of the country, Maurice divides his time between his office and apartment in the French Quarter of New Orleans and his house high in the mountains near Silver Cliff, Colorado. Licensed to practice before the highest courts of three states and the District of Columbia, Mr. Franks is a member of the bars of some fifteen federal courts, including the Supreme Court of the United States. He is the author of numerous scholarly articles on the law; one of his law journal articles recently was cited by the United States Court of Appeals at Philadelphia as the basis for a far-reaching decision involving class actions.

Big Bestsellers from SIGNET

☐ **THE GREEK TREASURE by Irving Stone.**
(#E7211—$2.25)

☐ **THE KITCHEN SINK PAPERS by Mike McGrady.**
(#J7212—$1.95)

☐ **THE GATES OF HELL by Harrison Salisbury.**
(#E7213—$2.25)

☐ **TERMS OF ENDEARMENT by Larry McMurtry.**
(#J7173—$1.95)

☐ **SAVAGE EDEN by Constance Gluyas.** (#J7171—$1.95)

☐ **ROSE: MY LIFE IN SERVICE by Rosina Harrison.**
(#J7174—$1.95)

☐ **THE FINAL FIRE by Dennis Smith.** (#J7141—$1.95)

☐ **SOME KIND OF HERO by James Kirkwood.**
(#J7142—$1.95)

☐ **A ROOM WITH DARK MIRRORS by Velda Johnston.**
(#W7143—$1.50)

☐ **THE HOMOSEXUAL MATRIX by C. A. Tripp.**
(#E7172—$2.50)

☐ **CBS: Reflections in a Bloodshot Eye by Robert Metz.**
(#E7115—$2.25)

☐ **'SALEM'S LOT by Stephen King.** (#J7112—$1.95)

☐ **CARRIE by Stephen King.** (#E6410—$1.75)

☐ **FATU-HIVA: Back to Nature by Thor Heyerdahl.**
(#J7113—$1.95)

More Big Bestsellers from SIGNET